CLASSIC STITCHING

25 Beautiful Projects

Adopt-A-Book

Purchase of this book was made possible by a

Generous Borrower

October—December 2015

CLASSIC STITCHING

25 Beautiful Projects

ANNA ELIZABETH DRAEGER

KALMBACH BOOKS

Kalmbach Books
21027 Crossroads Circle
Waukesha, Wisconsin 53186
www.JewelryandBeadingStore.com

Published in 2015
19 18 17 16 15   1 2 3 4 5

Manufactured in China

ISBN: 978-1-62700-148-9
EISBN: 978-1-62700-149-6

The material in this book has appeared previously in *Bead&Button* and *Bead Style* magazines. *Bead&Button* and *Bead Style* are registered trademarks.

Editor: Karin Van Voorhees
Book Design: Lisa Schroeder
Illustrator: Kellie Jaeger
Photographers: William Zuback and James Forbes

Library of Congress Control Number: 2014958384

CONTENTS

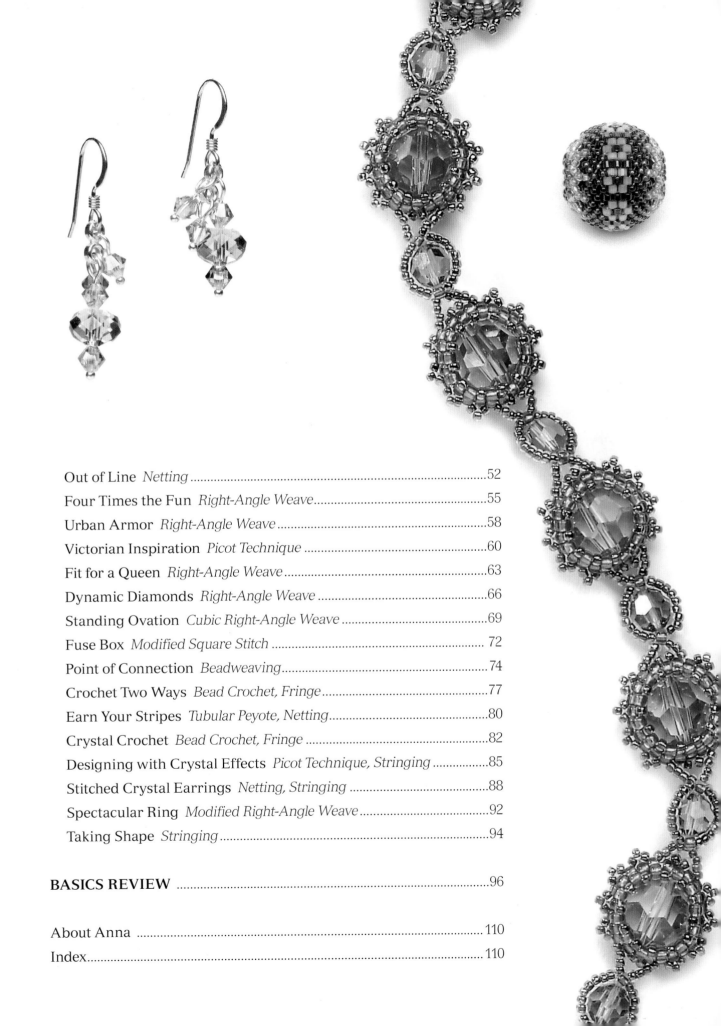

MEETANNA

Experimentation, a desire to teach, and a love of "sparkly stuff" propels this noted designer, author, teacher, and artist as she advances her beadwork.

You may recognize Anna Elizabeth Draeger's work by its signature sparkle. Her crystal-laden projects have appeared over the last decade in *Bead&Button*, her five published books, and her numerous class offerings. Perhaps most importantly to Anna, her impeccable designs and technical expertise have earned her a loyal following of readers and students. Anna's recognition in the beading world seems unsurprising for a woman who, as a child, always liked to collect "sparkly stuff," including her artist-grandmother's rhinestone jewelry.

Collecting jewelry turned to making it out of necessity when Anna's sister Amy asked her to remake their grandmother's beaded American Indian collar, which had becomes too fragile to wear. So, without knowing anything about beading stitches, Anna replicated the collar, using seed beads and sewing thread. She learned about formal stitches when she picked up the first issue of *Bead&Button* in 1994.

After stitching the collar, Anna continued to work with seed beads, replicating beaded pieces and interpreting other types of jewelry in seed beads. She was most drawn to American Indian pieces, which used seed beads in primary colors.

Peyote, netting, and herringbone are among Anna's favorite stitches. She mainly designs bracelets using crystals because relatively quick, precise designs are easier for her students and readers to learn (and because she loves crystals).

By the time Anna was a senior in high school, she'd been beading with seed beads for three years. While on winter break, she stepped into a bead store and discovered crystals. "Whatever money I had, I used up right then and there," she says.

Her pieces are predominantly monochromatic and designed with such precision that they look more intricate than they really are.

This compiled collection of projects spans Anna's many years as Associate Editor for Bead & Button *magazine. Never short of ideas, this prolific artist has published projects at all levels incorporating many stitches and diverse materials. This collection truly has something for everyone.*

GETTING STARTED

Expert Advice ... Just Ask Anna!

The best way to master anything is to jump in and spend hours working on it. A little advanced preparation can reduce frustration. Here are a few tips to help you:

- Take some time to review the basics before starting a project; it will help you achieve quick success. In this book, stitches used are noted by the material list, and a Basics Review begins on p. 96.
- Before you begin a beading project, find out all you can about the materials you will be using. Learn the differences in threads and needles, and which will work best with the kind of beads used in the project.
- Know your tools. My dad is a big believer in "the right tool for the right job," and he ingrained the notion in my head. With all the cool beading tools on the market, it pays to research each one. If you stick with beading, you will want the best tools that you can afford. And if you don't stick with beading (which is, of course, unlikely), it will be easier to sell a decent set of tools.

While you're working

- Work with comfortable lengths of thread (a length that you can manage without tangling it around yourself and everything around you), and position the needle about five inches from the end of the thread. Too much thread doubled over the needle will cause tangles.
- When you add thread, weave the new thread into the existing beadwork, and exit where your old thread left off. This sounds simple, but it is important to exit the same direction as your old thread. You don't want to stitch in the wrong direction!
- When beading with sharp beads or crystals, pull the thread straight through the hole of the bead. If you pull it at an angle, you may weaken the thread or scrape the nylon coating off of the beading wire, compromising the integrity of your finished piece.

Finishing

- When you end your final thread, retrace the thread path before knotting the thread. Sew through the beads that attach the clasp and the last few rows or stitches to lock the thread in place. It is more important to weave through the beadwork than to tie knots (although I do both). If you tie a knot or two without retracing the thread path, and the knot comes undone, your beads could start falling off. But if you have woven through your work repeatedly and the knot comes undone, you will notice a tail sticking out, giving you the opportunity to fix the problem before your piece starts falling apart.
- Practice techniques, such as tying knots and crimping, until you are satisfied with your results.
- A small dot of flexible glue (such as G-S Hypo Cement) on the final knot of your project can help secure it.
- Get help. If you are getting frustrated, ask for help at a local bead store or take a class. Search online at BeadAndButton.com for videos on techniques, online basics, an extensive online glossary, and many other resources available to make beading easier.
- Relax, and enjoy your time beading. With all the stress of everyday life, beading should be a way to unwind and express your creative side.

HOW TO USE THIS BOOK

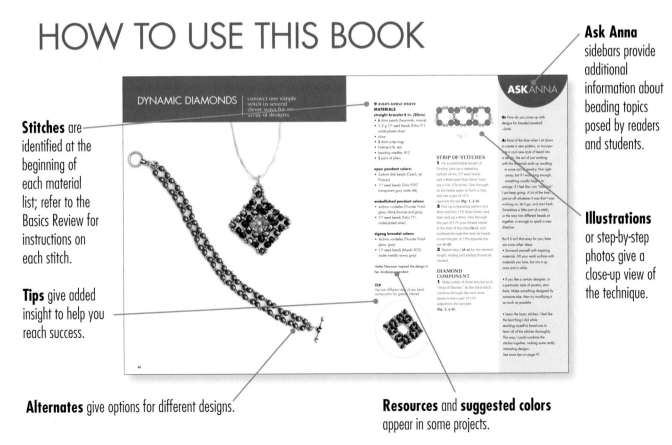

Stitches are identified at the beginning of each material list; refer to the Basics Review for instructions on each stitch.

Tips give added insight to help you reach success.

Ask Anna sidebars provide additional information about beading topics posed by readers and students.

Illustrations or step-by-step photos give a close-up view of the technique.

Alternates give options for different designs.

Resources and **suggested colors** appear in some projects.

PROJECTS

Link plain and embellished
dimensional rings to create
nature-inspired accessories.

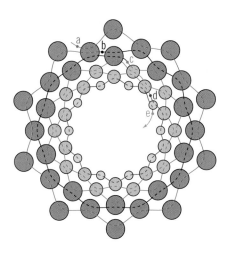

Fig. 1

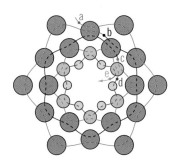

Fig. 2

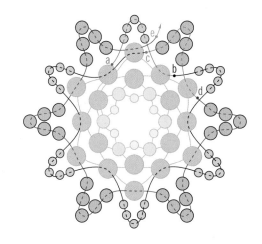

Fig. 3

BUDS

1 On 1 yd. (.9 m) of Fireline, attach a stop bead, leaving a 6-in. (15cm) tail. Pick up 20 8º seed beads, and sew through the first 8º again to form a ring **(fig. 1, a–b)**. These beads will shift to create the first two rounds as round 3 is added.

2 Work a round of tubular peyote stitch using 8ºs, and step up through the first 8º added in this round **(b–c)**.

3 Work two rounds using 11º seed beads, working with medium tension, and stepping up after each round **(c–d)**.

4 Work a round using 15º seed beads **(d–e)**. Retrace the last two rounds, and sew through the beadwork to exit an 8º in the outer round of 8ºs.

5 Repeat steps 3 and 4 on this side of the bud, making the beadwork curl into a tire shape. Exit an 8º in the center round along the outer edge. Don't end the working thread. Remove the stop bead, and end the tail.

6 Make a total of seven buds.

FLOWERS

1 On 1½ yd. (1.4 m) of Fireline, attach a stop bead, leaving a 6-in. (15cm) tail. Pick up 12 8ºs, and sew through the first 8º again to form a ring **(fig. 2, a–b)**.

2 Work a round using 8ºs, and step up through the first 8º added in this round **(b–c)**.

3 Work a round using 11ºs, and step up through the first 11º added in this round **(c–d)**.

4 Work a round using 15ºs **(d–e)**. Retrace the last two rounds, and exit an 8º in the outer round of 8ºs.

5 Repeat steps 3 and 4 on this side of the bud, making the beadwork curl into a tire shape. Exit an 8º in the center round along the outer edge. Remove the stop bead, and end the tail.

6 Using the working thread, pick up five 15ºs, and sew through the next 8º in the round **(fig. 3, a–b)**. Repeat to complete the round, and step up through the adjacent 8º in the next round **(b–c)**.

7 Pick up five 11ºs, and sew through the next 8º in the round **(c–d)**. Repeat to complete the round **(d–e)**. Retrace the thread path

MATERIALS

bracelet 7½ in. (19.1cm) or necklace 15½ –19½ in. (39.4–49.5cm)

- 4–5 g 8º seed beads
- 3–4 g 11º seed beads
- 2–3 g 15º seed beads
- clasp
- 8–12 in. (20–30cm) decorative chain (for necklace)
- 2–4 6mm jump rings
- pair of earring wires (for earrings)
- Fireline 6 lb. test
- beading needles, #12
- 2 pairs of pliers
- wire cutters (for necklace)

TIP

Stitch the components together to make a bracelet. For a necklace, extend the bracelet length with your favorite chain.

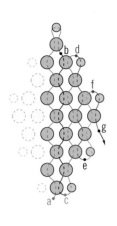

Fig. 4

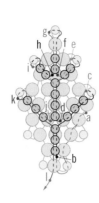

Fig. 5

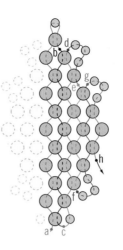

Fig. 6

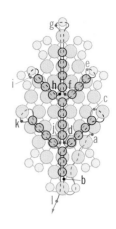

Fig. 7

through the first two rounds of 8ºs, tying a few half-hitch knots to secure the thread; don't end the working thread. Exit an 8º in the center round along the outer edge.

8 Make a total of four flowers.

9 To make the center flower: Use the working thread from a bud, and repeat steps 6 and 7.

NARROW LEAF
Base

1 On 1 yd. (.9 m) of Fireline, pick up nine 11ºs and a 15º, leaving a 10-in. (25cm) tail. Skip the 15º, and sew back through the last 11º **(fig. 4, a–b)**. The 11ºs shift to create the first two rows as the third row is added.

1 flower + 2 leaves + 1 earring finding x 2 = a cute pair of earrings!

2 Work the following rows in flat even-count peyote stitch:

Row 3: Four stitches using one 11º per stitch **(b–c)**.

Row 4: One stitch using a 15º and three stitches using 11ºs **(c–d)**.

Row 5: One stitch using a 15º and two stitches using 11ºs **(d–e)**.

Row 6: One stitch using a 15º and one stitch using an 11º **(e–f)**.

Row 7: Pick up a 15º, and sew back through the 11º in the previous row **(f–g)**.

3 Using the tail, work rows 4–7 on the other side of the leaf. End the tail.

Veins

1 Using the working thread, sew through the next three 11ºs, the 15º at the bottom of the leaf, and the adjacent 11º so the needle is pointing toward the top of the leaf **(fig. 5, a–b)**.

2 Pick up six 15ºs, sew through the third 15º along one edge of the leaf **(b–c)**, and sew back through the last three 15ºs picked up **(c–d)**. Pick up six 15ºs, sew through the fourth 15º along the edge of the leaf **(d–e)**, and sew back through the last two 15ºs picked up **(e–f)**. Pick up two 15ºs, sew through the 11º and 15º at the top of the leaf **(f–g)**,

and sew back through the 11º and the last two 15ºs picked up **(g–h)**. Pick up two 15ºs, and sew through the fourth 15º along the other edge of the leaf **(h–i)**. Sew back through the last two 15ºs picked up and the next four center 15ºs, working back toward the bottom of the leaf **(i–j)**. Pick up three 15ºs, and sew through the third 15º along this edge of the leaf **(j–k)**. Sew back through the last three 15ºs picked up, the next three center 15ºs, and the bottom 11º **(k–l)**. Don't end the working thread.

WIDE LEAF
Base

1 On 1 yd. (.9 m) of Fireline, pick up 11 11ºs and a 15º, leaving a 10-in. (25cm) tail. Skip the 15º, and sew back through the last 11º **(fig. 6, a–b)**.

2 Work the following rows in flat even-count peyote stitch:

Row 3: Five stitches using one 11º per stitch **(b–c)**.

Row 4: One stitch using a 15º and four stitches using 11ºs **(c–d)**.

Row 5: One stitch using three 15ºs **(d–e)** and three stitches using 11ºs **(e–f)**.

Row 6: One stitch using three 15ºs and two stitches using 11ºs **(f–g)**.

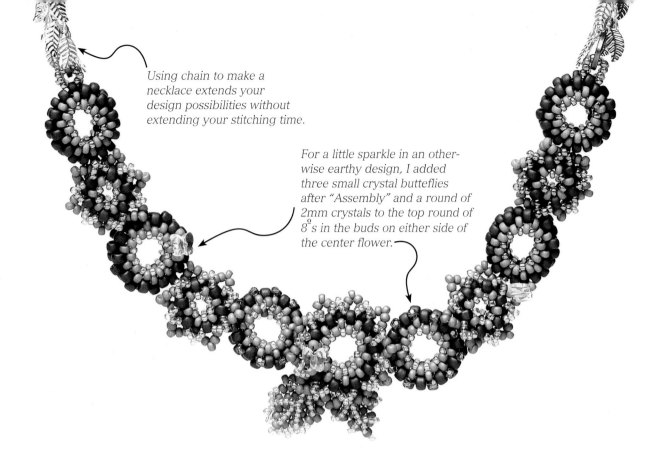

Using chain to make a necklace extends your design possibilities without extending your stitching time.

For a little sparkle in an otherwise earthy design, I added three small crystal butterflies after "Assembly" and a round of 2mm crystals to the top round of 8ºs in the buds on either side of the center flower.

Row 7: One stitch using three 15ºs and one stitch using an 11º **(g–h)**.

3 Using the tail, work rows 4–7 on the leaf's other side. End the tail.

Veins

1 Using the working thread, sew through the next three 11ºs, the 15º at the bottom of the leaf, and the adjacent 11º so the needle is pointing toward the top of the leaf **(fig. 7, a–b)**.

2 Pick up seven 15ºs, sew through the 11º added in the last row along one edge of the leaf **(b–c)**, and sew back through the last four 15ºs picked up **(c–d)**. Pick up seven 15ºs, skip an 11º and two 15ºs along the edge of the leaf, and sew through the next 15º **(d–e)**. Sew back through the last three 15ºs picked up **(e–f)**. Pick up four 15ºs, and sew through the 11º and 15º at the top of the leaf **(f–g)**. Sew back through the 11º and the last four 15ºs picked up **(g–h)**. Pick up three 15ºs, skip two 11ºs and three 15ºs along the other

edge of the leaf, and sew through the next 15º **(h–i)**. Sew back through the last three 15ºs picked up and the next four center 15ºs, working back toward the bottom of the leaf **(i–j)**. Pick up four 15ºs, skip two 15ºs and an 11º along this edge of the leaf, and sew through the next 11º **(j–k)**. Sew back through the last four 15ºs picked up, the next three center 15ºs, and the bottom 11º **(k–l)**. Don't end the working thread.

ASSEMBLY

1 Using the working thread from a bud, pick up nine 15ºs, and sew through the 8º your thread exited at the start of this step to form a ring. Repeat to create a second ring of 15ºs next to the first. Retrace the thread path of both rings, then sew through the beadwork to exit an 8º on the opposite side of the bud. This 8º will be a connection point.

2 On a flower component, locate the 8º opposite the 8º the working thread is exiting. This will be the next connection point. Using the

working thread from the bud component, sew through the connection point 8ºs on the two components, following a ladder stitch thread path. Retrace the thread path a few times, and end the working thread from the bud.

3 Repeat step 2, alternating bud and flower components, using the largest flower in the center. After connecting the last bud, make two rings of 15ºs as in step 1, opposite the last connection point.

4 Using the working thread from the leaves, attach the leaves to the center flower component.

5 To make a bracelet: With a jump ring, attach half of the clasp to the rings of 15ºs on one end of the beadwork. Repeat on the other end. To make a necklace: Cut two pieces of chain to the desired length. With a jump ring, attach an end link of one chain and the rings of 15ºs on one end of the beadwork. With a jump ring attach half of the clasp to the remaining end link of chain. Repeat on the other side of the necklace.

TWISTED CUFF

Use graduated bead sizes to create a natural twist.

● TUBULAR PEYOTE
MATERIALS
bracelet 9 in. (23cm)
- seed beads
    - 10 g 6º
    - 15 g 8º
    - 20 g 11º
- 10 g 10º triangles
- bracelet-diameter memory wire
- Fireline 6 lb. test
- beading needles, #12
- sturdy roundnose pliers
- memory wire cutters

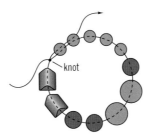

Fig. 1

Fig. 2

1 On a comfortable length of Fireline, pick up five 11º seed beads, one 8º seed bead, two 6º seed beads, two 8ºs, and two 10º triangles. Tie the beads into a ring with a square knot, leaving a 10-in. (25cm) tail. Sew through the first two 11ºs again **(fig. 1)**.
2 Working in tubular peyote stitch, pick up one bead per stitch in the following order: an 11º, an 11º, an 8º, a 6º, an 8º, and a triangle. Step up through the first 11º added in the round **(fig. 2)**.
3 Repeat step 2 until your tube is 1 in. (2.5cm) shorter than the desired length. You may want to slide the beadwork over a small dowel to help form the first few rounds of the tube.
4 Work three rounds with one 11º per stitch. Work a decrease round with 11ºs, adding an 11º every other stitch. Work one more round,

adding an 11º between each pair of 11ºs in the previous round. Retrace the thread path of the last round to reinforce it, and pull the beads into a tight ring. Secure the working thread with a few half-hitch knots, and trim.
5 Cut a piece of memory wire to the length of your tube. With sturdy roundnose pliers, make a small simple loop on each end to prevent the wire ends from poking out of the beadwork. Insert the memory wire into the tube. If the bracelet doesn't hold its shape, insert a second piece of memory wire.
6 Using the tail, repeat step 4 on the other end of the bracelet.

TIP
To make a necklace, simply make a longer tube, and insert a length of necklace-diameter memory wire into the tube.

Q: *What is the best way to end/add thread to my stitched project?* -Gary

A: Adding and ending thread properly is crucial. Without it, you will compromise the integrity of your work and/or end up with bulky areas of thread and knots.

Make a clean connection by stitching back through the beadwork that you have already completed, following the thread path, tying a few half-hitch knots along the way, and then trimming the thread. To secure a new thread, weave the thread in the same manner, making sure to exit the beadwork in the same place you left off, leaving another short tail to tie in. (Secure the short tail right away so it doesn't get in the way as you continue to work.)

Another method is to stop beading when your working thread is about 6 in. (15cm) long. Cut a new length of thread, and tie the new thread (leaving a 6-in. tail) to the old tail with a surgeon's knot. Work a few stitches until the knot is hidden in the beadwork. Leave the tails sticking out. When the knot is hidden, thread a needle on one tail at a time and end them as explained previously.

What about dotting the knot with G-S Hypo Cement? If you weave through the beadwork enough, you don't need the glue. Additionally, it may stiffen your beadwork in that area. Finishing techniques can take just as much time to get comfortable with as the stitches, so practice them just as you would the stitches.

LUXURIOUS LINKS

Mimic expensive, chunky metal chain with cylinders and seed beads worked in peyote stitch.

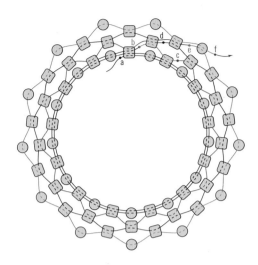

Fig. 1

● TUBULAR PEYOTE

MATERIALS

bracelet 7 in. (18cm)

- 10 g 11º cylinder beads
- 8 g 5º seed beads
- clasp
- 2 5mm inside diameter (ID) jump rings
- 4mm ID jump ring (optional)
- Fireline 6 lb. test
- beading needles, #12
- chainnose pliers
- roundnose pliers

1 On 1 yd. (.9 m) of Fireline, pick up an alternating pattern of an 11º cylinder bead and a 15º seed bead until you have 26 beads, leaving a 6-in. (15cm) tail. Sew through all the beads again to form a ring, and exit the first cylinder strung **(fig. 1, a–b)**.

2 Work a round of tubular peyote using cylinders: Pick up a cylinder, skip a 15º in the ring, and sew through the next cylinder **(b–c)**. Repeat to complete the round, and step up through the first cylinder in the new round **(c–d)**.

3 Work a round of tubular peyote using cylinders, and step up through the first cylinder in the new round **(d–e)**.

4 Work a round of tubular peyote using 15ºs **(e–f)**; pull the round snug.

5 Sew back through each round to reinforce the link, working back to the tail.

6 Tie the working thread and the tail together with a surgeon's knot. Sew through several beads with each tail, and trim.

A

7 To make subsequent links, repeat steps 1–6, but before forming the ring in step 1, pass the row of cylinders through the previous ring **(photo a)**.

8 Continue to make links until your chain is the desired length, minus the length of the clasp.

TIP

If you are using a toggle and loop clasp, you may have to use an extra 4mm jump ring to attach the toggle bar. This extra length will allow the toggle bar to pivot enough to get through the loop.

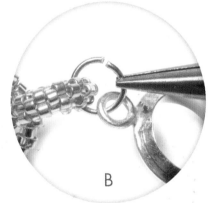

B

9 Open a 5mm jump ring. Slide the last link of the beaded chain and one half of the clasp on the jump ring **(photo b)**, and close the jump ring. Repeat with the other half of the clasp.

CRYSTAL MEDALLIONS

Lacy medallions studded with crystals lend a lightness to this piece.

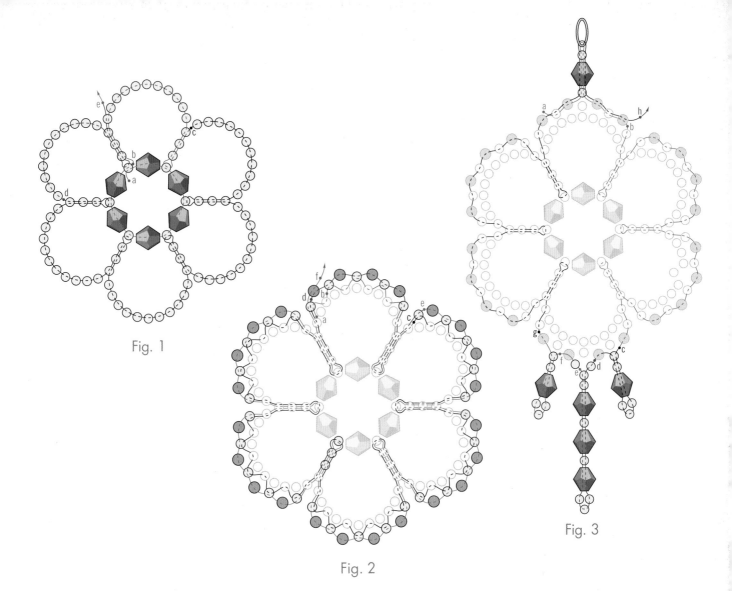

Fig. 1

Fig. 2

Fig. 3

1 On a 2-yd. (1.8m) length of thread, pick up a repeating pattern of a 15º seed bead and a 4mm bicone crystal six times, leaving a 6-in. (15cm) tail. Sew through the first 15º to form a ring **(fig. 1, a–b)**.

2 Pick up 17 15ºs, and sew through the next 15º in the ring. Sew back through the last three 15ºs **(b–c)**.

3 Pick up 14 15ºs. Sew through the next 15º in the ring and back through the last three 15ºs. Repeat three times **(c–d)**.

4 Pick up 11 15ºs, sew through the first three 15ºs from step 2, and sew through the next 15º in the ring. Sew back through the first four 15ºs from step 2 **(d–e)**.

5 Pick up a 15º, skip a 15º, and sew through the next 15º **(fig. 2, a–b)**. Continue in peyote stitch for four

stitches. Then sew through the next three 15ºs, the next 15º in the ring, and back through the last three 15ºs. Continue through the 15º on the next loop **(b–c)**. Repeat this step five times, exiting the first 15º added in this step **(c–d)**.

6 Work the next four stitches of peyote with 11ºs, and sew through to the next loop **(d–e)**. Repeat on each loop, and exit the first 11º added in this round **(e–f)**.

7 Sew through the next 15º and 11º. Pick up a 15º, a 4mm, a 15º, and a soldered jump ring. Skip the soldered jump ring, and sew back through the 15º, the 4mm, the 15º, and the next three beads **(fig. 3, a–b)**.

8 Follow the thread path around the outer edge of the loops to the

● **PEYOTE, STRINGING, WIREWORK**
MATERIALS
necklace 16 in. (41cm)

• Swarovski crystals or pearls
    28 6mm round or bicone
    68 4mm bicone
• seed beads
    4 g 11º
    6 g 15º
• clasp
• 8 in. (20cm) 20- or 22-gauge wire
• **6** soldered jump rings
• **2** crimp beads
• Nymo D or Fireline 6 lb. test
• flexible beading wire, .014
• beading needles, #13
• chainnose pliers
• crimping pliers
• roundnose pliers
• wire cutters

opposite side of the pendant, exiting at **point c**. Add three fringes to the bottom loop as follows:

Fringe 1: Pick up two 15ºs, a 4mm, and three 15ºs. Skip the last three 15ºs, and sew back through the 4mm and the two 15ºs. Sew through the next 11º **(c–d)**.

Fringe 2: Pick up three 15ºs, a 4mm, a 15º, a 4mm, a 15º, a 4mm, and three 15ºs. Skip the last three 15ºs, and sew back through the beads, skipping the first 15º **(d–e)**. Pick up a 15º, and sew through the next 11º **(e–f)**.

Fringe 3: Repeat fringe 1 **(f–g)**.

9 Follow the thread path back to the top loop. Reinforce the beads from step 7 with a second thread path **(g–h)**. End the thread and tail.

MEDALLIONS

Make the medallions by following the steps for the pendant, but add a soldered jump ring on opposite sides and eliminate the fringe. Make two medallions.

CRYSTAL LINKS

Cut a 4-in. (10cm) length of wire. Make a plain loop on one end. String a 4mm, a 6mm bicone crystal, and a 4mm. Make a plain loop on the other end. Make a second crystal link.

ASSEMBLY

1 Open one loop on a crystal link, and attach it to the pendant's soldered jump ring. Close the loop.

Open the loop on the other end, and attach it to a medallion. Repeat with the second crystal link and medallion.

2 Cut a 16-in. (41cm) piece of beading wire. On the wire, center 17 15ºs and the available soldered jump ring of one medallion. String an 11º over both wire ends to create a loop of 15ºs around the soldered jump ring **(photo a)**.

3 String an assortment of beads and 4mm and 6mm crystals over each end, occasionally putting both ends through a 4mm **(photo b)**.

4 When the strand is about 4 in. (10cm) short of the desired length, string a crimp bead and one half of the clasp over both ends. Take both ends back through the crimp bead, and tighten the loop. Crimp the crimp bead.

5 Repeat steps 1–4 on the other side of the necklace.

TIP
To continue the floral motif, make enough medallions for the entire length of the necklace's sides (eight in total). Be sure to make enough crystal links to connect them as well.

A

B

COCKTAIL HOUR

Tubular peyote stitch and netting surround a crystal drop, creating a retro-style cocktail ring.

● TUBULAR PEYOTE, NETTING, CROSSWEAVE
MATERIALS
ring size 7
- Swarovski crystals
    - 11x5.5mm faceted teardrop
    - **6** 4mm bicones
    - **22** 3mm bicones
- seed beads
    - 2 g 11º
    - 2 g 15º
- Fireline 6 lb. test
- flexible beading wire, .010
- beading needles, #12
- chainnose pliers
- wire cutters
- G-S Hypo Cement (optional)

TOP

1 On 1 yd. (.9 m) of Fireline, leave a 12-in. (30cm) tail, and pick up an 11º seed bead, the crystal teardrop, and an 11º. Skip the last 11º, and sew back through the teardrop and the 11º in the opposite direction **(photo a)**.

2 Pick up a 15º seed bead, an 11º, and a 15º, and sew through the opposite 11º **(photo b)**. Repeat once to create a ring around the base of the teardrop **(photo c)**.

3 Working toward the teardrop's larger end, pick up an 11º, skip the next 15º in the ring, and sew through the next 11º **(photo d)**. Continue working in tubular peyote stitch for the next three stitches. Step up through the first 11º added in this round **(photo e)**.

4 Pick up a 15º, an 11º, and a 15º. Skip the next 11º, and sew through the next 11º in the previous round **(photo f)**. Continue in tubular netting stitch, adding three beads per stitch for the next three stitches. The needle should be exiting the first 11º in the previous round **(photo g)**.

5 Pick up a 15º and sew through the next 11º **(photo h)**. Continue in tubular peyote with 15ºs for the next seven stitches. The number of beads in the round will increase. Step up through the first 15º added in this round **(photo i)**.

6 Work a round of tubular peyote using 11ºs, a round of 15ºs, a round of 11ºs, and one last round of 15ºs, stepping up after each round. Sew through the last two rounds to

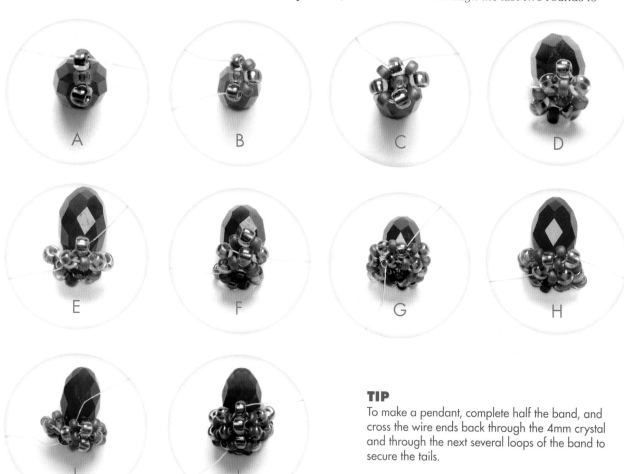

A B C D

E F G H

I J

TIP
To make a pendant, complete half the band, and cross the wire ends back through the 4mm crystal and through the next several loops of the band to secure the tails.

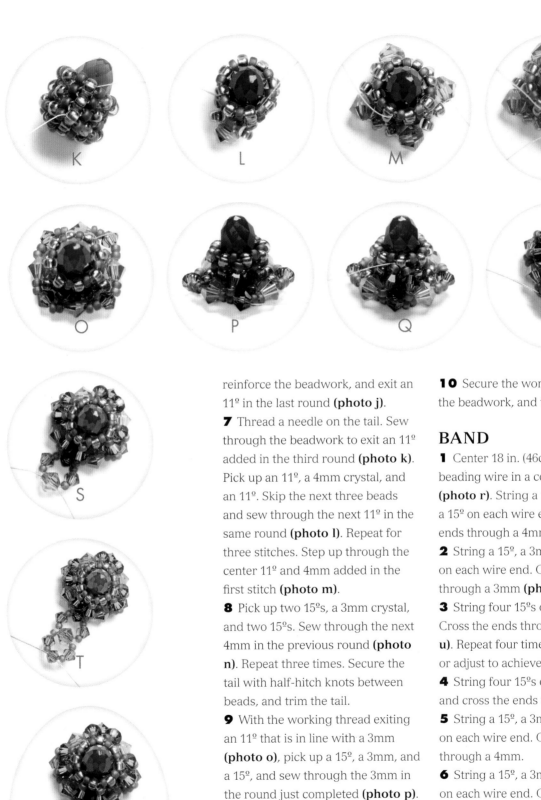

reinforce the beadwork, and exit an 11º in the last round **(photo j)**.

7 Thread a needle on the tail. Sew through the beadwork to exit an 11º added in the third round **(photo k)**. Pick up an 11º, a 4mm crystal, and an 11º. Skip the next three beads and sew through the next 11º in the same round **(photo l)**. Repeat for three stitches. Step up through the center 11º and 4mm added in the first stitch **(photo m)**.

8 Pick up two 15ºs, a 3mm crystal, and two 15ºs. Sew through the next 4mm in the previous round **(photo n)**. Repeat three times. Secure the tail with half-hitch knots between beads, and trim the tail.

9 With the working thread exiting an 11º that is in line with a 3mm **(photo o)**, pick up a 15º, a 3mm, and a 15º, and sew through the 3mm in the round just completed **(photo p)**. Pick up a 15º, a 3mm, and a 15º. Sew back through the 11º your thread exited at the beginning of this step **(photo q)**, and through four beads to exit the 11º that is lined up with the next 3mm. Repeat three times.

10 Secure the working thread in the beadwork, and trim.

BAND

1 Center 18 in. (46cm) of beading wire in a corner 3mm **(photo r)**. String a 15º, a 3mm, and a 15º on each wire end. Cross the ends through a 4mm **(photo s)**.

2 String a 15º, a 3mm, and a 15º on each wire end. Cross the ends through a 3mm **(photo t)**.

3 String four 15ºs on each wire end. Cross the ends through a 15º **(photo u)**. Repeat four times for a size 7 ring or adjust to achieve the desired size.

4 String four 15ºs on each wire end, and cross the ends through a 3mm.

5 String a 15º, a 3mm, and a 15º on each wire end. Cross the ends through a 4mm.

6 String a 15º, a 3mm, and a 15º on each wire end. Cross the ends through the 3mm on the opposite side of the ring top.

7 Weave the ends back through the band. Tie a half-hitch knot between two beads, go through the next bead, and trim the tails. Place a dot of glue next to where you trimmed.

DELICATE DOMES

Flat circular peyote stitch creates curved components; a subtle shift of bead sizes allows the domed shape to emerge.

● CIRCULAR PEYOTE
MATERIALS
bracelet 7 in. (18cm)

- 5–7 g 10º cylinder beads (Miyuki 0007, metallic brown iris)
- 2–3 g 11º seed beads (Toho 999, gray-lined crystal AB)
- 2–3 g 11º cylinder beads (Miyuki 671, silver-lined variegated taupe)
- 1–2 g 15º seed beads (Miyuki 551, gilt-lined opal)
- clasp
- **2** 6mm jump rings
- Fireline 6 lb. test
- beading needles, #12
- **2** pairs of pliers

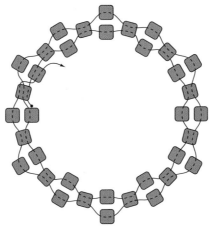

Fig. 1

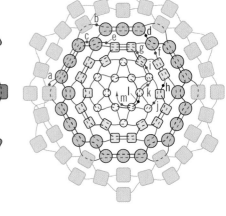

Fig. 2

1 On a comfortable length of Fireline, pick up 24 10º cylinder beads, leaving a 10-in. (25cm) tail. Work a round of circular peyote stitch using 10ºs. Exit a 10º along the inner edge of the ring **(fig. 1)**.

2 Pick up three 11º seed beads, skip the next three 10ºs, and sew through the following 10º along the inner edge of the ring **(fig. 2, a–b)**. The stitch will sit on top of the initial ring of peyote. Repeat this stitch to complete the round, and step up through the first three 11ºs picked up in this round **(b–c)**.

3 Pick up an 11º seed bead, and sew through the next three 11º seed beads in the previous round **(c–d)**. Repeat this stitch to complete the round, and step up through the first 11º seed bead picked up in this round **(d–e)**.

4 Pick up two 11º cylinder beads, and sew through the next 11º seed bead in the previous round **(e–f)**. Repeat this stitch to complete the round, and step up through the first two 11º cylinders picked up in this round **(f–g)**.

5 Pick up an 11º cylinder, and sew through the next two 11º cylinders in the previous round **(g–h)**. Repeat this stitch to complete the round, and step up through the first 11º cylinder picked up in this round **(h–i)**.

6 Pick up a 15º seed bead, and sew through the next 11º cylinder in the previous round **(i–j)**. Repeat this stitch to complete the round, and step up through the first 15º picked up in this round **(j–k)**. Work another round with 15ºs, sewing through the 15ºs in the previous round **(k–l)**.

7 Sew through the six 15ºs in the center ring to snug up the beads **(l–m)**.

8 Sew through the beadwork to exit a 10º along the outer edge of the initial ring. Pick up seven 10ºs, and sew through the outer-edge 10º to make a loop to attach the clasp. Retrace the thread path of the ring, skipping every other bead if desired to pull the ring into a

diamond shape. Sew through the beadwork to exit a 10º opposite the loop of 10ºs.

9 Pick up 23 10ºs, and sew through the 10º your thread exited at the start of this step. Sew through the next 10º in the new ring, and then work a round of peyote using 10ºs, exiting a 10º along the inner edge of the ring. Work as in steps 2–7 to complete the component, and then sew through the beadwork to exit the edge 10º opposite the previous join.

10 Repeat step 9 to complete the desired number of domed components, ending and adding thread as needed. After completing the last component, make a loop of 10ºs as in step 8 opposite the last join. End any remaining threads.

11 Open a jump ring, and attach half of the clasp to a loop of 10ºs on one end of the bracelet. Repeat on the other end.

TIPS
- Satin beads can have sharp holes that may wear down your thread as you work. To avoid breakage, work with shorter lengths of thread conditioned with wax or Thread Heaven.
- A single component would make a cute ring top, or you can work up a couple to create a pair of matching earrings. Steps 2–7 can be worked on the back surface of the initial ring of peyote to make a two-sided bauble that's adorable whether you're coming or going.

TUBE EARRINGS

Make tubes with bugle beads and bicones, then string the tubes on head pins for easy earrings.

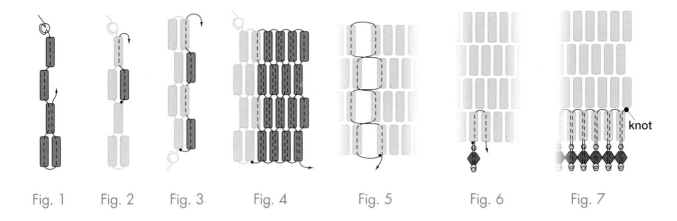

Fig. 1   Fig. 2   Fig. 3   Fig. 4   Fig. 5   Fig. 6   Fig. 7

knot

● **PEYOTE, FRINGE**

MATERIALS

earrings

- **2** 6mm bicone crystals
- **4mm** stopper bead
- **16** 3mm bicone crystals
- **48** 3mm (size 1) bugle beads
- **24** 15º seed beads
- **2** 4mm bead caps
- **2** 2-in. (5cm) head pins
- Fireline or Wildfire, 6 lb. test
- pair of earring wires
- chainnose and roundnose pliers
- diagonal wire cutters
- scissors
- beading needle, #12

1 For each earring: Cut a 1-yd. (.9 m) piece of Fireline or Wildfire and thread a needle. String a stop bead. Pick up five bugle beads and slide them up to the stop bead. Skip the last two beads and sew through the next with your needle pointing toward the tail. The two skipped beads should be parallel **(fig. 1)**.

2 Pick up a bugle, skip a bugle, and sew through the next bugle, exiting the same bead as the tail. This completes the first two rows of peyote **(fig. 2)**.

3 Turn the piece over so the tail is toward you. Pick up a bugle, skip the bead the thread is exiting, and sew through the next bead. Pick up a bead, skip a bead, and sew through the next bead **(fig. 3)**.

4 Repeat the pattern until there are six beads in each horizontal row **(fig. 4)**.

5 Roll the beaded strip into a tube and zigzag through alternate beads on the ends of each row. Exit a bead at the bottom of the tube **(fig. 5)**.

6 Pick up a 15º seed bead, a 3mm crystal, and a 15º. Slide the beads up to the tube, skip the 15º just strung, and sew back through the 3mm, the 15º, and the bead at the bottom of the tube. Sew through the next bead at the bottom of the tube **(fig. 6)**.

7 Repeat step 6 until you've made six short fringes at the bottom of the tube. Weave the thread back into the beaded tube, tie a square knot between two beads, and trim the thread. Remove the stop bead and end the tail **(fig. 7)**.

8 On a head pin, string a 6mm bicone crystal, a 3mm bicone, and enough 15ºs to fill the hole of the beaded tube. Slide the beaded tube over the 15ºs and string a bead cap and a 3mm bicone. Make a plain loop **(photo a)**.

9 Open the loop of an earring wire and attach the dangle. Close the loop **(photo b)**.

A

B

BACK & FORTH

A simple back-and-forth weave gives this bracelet a beautifully lush look. Once you get the rhythm, you'll be surprised how easy this is.

TIP

The key to this project is very fine, kink-resistant beading wire. The seed bead trios keep the wire taut as you weave.

MATERIALS

bracelet

- **19–25** 8mm round crystals
- **26–34** 4mm bicone crystals, color A
- **24–32** 4mm bicone crystals, color B
- 3 g 15º seed beads
- flexible beading wire, .010
- **2** crimp beads
- toggle clasp
- chainnose or crimping pliers
- diagonal wire cutters

Color notes

white

- 4mm white opal and crystal champagne
- 8mm sand opal AB

blue and red

- 8mm turquoise
- 4mm dark sapphire and dark red coral

light blue

- 8mm Pacific opal
- 4mm Pacific opal and air blue opal AB 2x

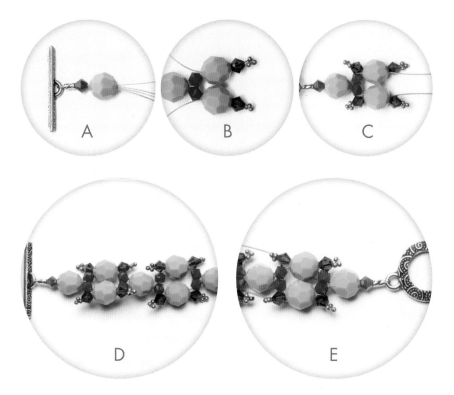

BRACELET

1 Cut two 36-in. (90cm) pieces of beading wire. Over both wires, center half of a toggle clasp, a crimp bead, a color A bicone crystal, and an 8mm crystal. With two of the strand ends together, go back through the crimp bead, the 4mm, and the 8mm and tighten the wires. Crimp the crimp bead and trim the excess wire **(photo a)**.

2 On each wire, string a color A bicone, an 8mm, a color B bicone, and three 15º seed beads. Go back through the color B bicone and the 8mm. Tighten the wires so the seed beads cluster **(photo b)**.

3 On each wire, string a color B bicone and three 15ºs. Go back through the color B bicone and the 8mm. Tighten the wires **(photo c)**.

4 On each wire, string a color A bicone. Over both wires, string an 8mm.

5 Repeat steps 2, 3, and 4 until the bracelet is within 1 in. (2.5cm) of the finished length **(photo d)**.

6 Over both wires, string an 8mm, a color A bicone, a crimp bead, and the remaining clasp half. Go back through the beads just strung. Tighten the wires. Crimp the crimp bead. Trim the excess wire **(photo e)**.

TIP

I used Twisted Tornado Crimp beads for the bracelets shown. Standard crimp beads will work too, but a secure crimp is critical for this bracelet because of the frequent wire tightening.

JUST PASSING THROUGH

Interlocking loops add interest and dimension to a crystal bracelet.

● CROSSWEAVE
MATERIALS
bracelet 8 in. (20cm)

- **61** 5mm bicone crystals, color A
- **61** 5mm bicone crystals, color B
- **1** g cylinder beads, color A
- **1** g cylinder beads, color B
- toggle clasp
- **2** medium cones
- **2** regular crimp beads
- **2** large (mighty) crimp beads
- flexible beading wire, .014–.015
- crimping pliers
- mighty crimping pliers
- wire cutters

TIP
Cut off two of the 2-in. (5cm) tails from step 1 to use regular size crimps in steps 2 and 10.

1 Cut four 1-yd. (.9m) pieces of beading wire. String a regular crimp bead over all four strands, 2 in. (5cm) from the ends. Crimp the crimp bead **(photo a)**.

2 String a cone, a large crimp bead, and half the clasp over the tail end of the wires, covering the regular crimp. Go back through the large crimp bead, tighten the loop, and crimp the crimp bead **(photo b)** with the mighty crimping pliers. Trim the tails as close to the crimp bead as possible.

3 String a color A crystal over all four wires and slide it into the cone **(photo c)**.

4 Divide the wires into two pairs. Working with one pair of wires, string the following on each wire: a color A cylinder bead, an A crystal, an A cylinder, an A crystal, and an A cylinder. Cross these wires through

another A crystal to complete the first ring **(photo d)**.

5 Repeat step 4 using the same pair of wires and As **(photo e)** until you have a total of 12 rings. Temporarily secure the tails and set aside.

6 Using the second pair of wires, string the following on each wire: a color B cylinder, a B crystal, and a B cylinder. Cross the wires through a B crystal. Pass the wire closest to the first color A ring through that ring **(photo f)**.

7 Bring that same wire back through the next color A ring to start the next B ring. On each wire, string the following: a B cylinder, a B crystal, a B cylinder, a B crystal, and a B cylinder. Cross the wires through a B crystal. Pass the wire closest to the next color A ring through that ring **(photo g)**.

E

F

G

H

I

Q: What can I do with leftover wire and beading wire?
–Erica

A: Recycle, recycle, recycle...I have been saving bits of beading wire for a very long time now: Whenever I was left with a 5-in. (13 cm) piece of beading wire at the end of a spool, or overestimated how much I'd need for a project, I'd make a loop with the wire and wrap one end around the other a few times to hold it in place. Then, I'd throw it in a little bag with about 25 other ringlets of colorful beading wire. Until now, that bag was just something I'd move from one place to the next, but I decided to make some earrings to use up the scraps.

I strung a few top-drilled crystals and some beads on one of the shorter scraps, then I crossed the ends through two crimp beads. I repeated this with two more leftover pieces, each one slightly longer than the previous one, crossing the wire ends through the same two crimps as the first loop. Leaving a little space between the two crimps, I crimped the crimp beads, and covered them with crimp covers. To finish up, I opened a loop of an earring finding, and attached it between the two crimp covers. So easy and so quick!

8 Repeat step 7 ten more times. String a B cylinder, a B crystal, and a B cylinder on each wire.

9 Pick up the other pair of wires, and gather the four strands. String an A crystal and a regular crimp bead over them. Crimp the crimp bead **(photo h)**.

10 String a cone, a large crimp bead, and the other clasp half over all four strands. Take the ends back through the large crimp bead **(photo i)**. Crimp the crimp bead as before and trim the tails close to the crimp.

CRYSTAL KISSES

A double layer of
bicones adds depth
to a simple weave.

● **CROSSWEAVE**

MATERIALS

bracelet

- **210–248** 3mm bicone crystals,
  106–126 color A, **104–122** color B
- 5 g 15º seed beads
- flexible beading wire, .010
- **2** 7mm jump rings
- crimp bead
- toggle clasp
- **2** pairs of pliers
- diagonal wire cutters
- crimping pliers (optional)

earrings

- **16** 3mm bicone crystals,
  8 color A, **8** color B
- **14** 15º seed beads
- beading thread
- **2** 7mm jump rings
- pair of marquise earring wires
- **2** pairs of chainnose pliers, or
  chainnose and roundnose pliers
- beading needle
- scissors

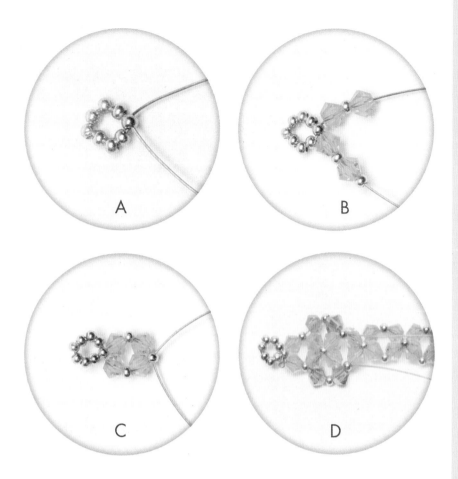

A

B

C

D

Q: When I finish crimping the project there is too much play in the wire; especially with bracelets. I just can't get the tension correct. The crimps are tight, the wire isn't slipping loose after crimping. I know the wire doesn't stretch, so I'm doing something incorrectly. Help! –Martha

A: It sounds to me as if you are allowing too much room between the components.

When you are crimping, you have to leave just the right amount of room so the bracelet or necklace can curve without being too stiff, yet not have too much space between the components.

When I finish stringing a bracelet or necklace, I lay out the strand on my work surface, and finish one end first. That is the easy part. Then I string the crimp bead and other half of the clasp on the other end. I play with the tension a bit, usually I make it as tight as possible, then bend the jewelry into the shape it will be when it is worn. I allow the beads to push the crimp bead along as I make sure the curve isn't too tight or stiff. Then I lay out the jewelry in a straight line again, and crimp the crimp bead. I usually cover my crimp beads with crimp covers, which led me to another fix. If you have too much slack, you can close an extra crimp cover over the wire right next to the crimped bead, filling in some of the space, or you can try to hide it within the design somewhere.

BRACELET

1 To make the color A strand: Cut a 3-ft. (91cm) piece of beading wire. Center eight 15º seed beads. String one end through the eighth bead in the opposite direction. Go through all the beads again to reinforce the ring **(photo a)**.

2 On each end, string a color A bicone crystal, a 15º, and an A. On one end, string a 15º **(photo b)**.

3 a String the other end through the last 15º, in the opposite direction **(photo c)**.

b Repeat steps 2 and 3a until the bracelet is within 1 in. (2.5 cm) of the finished length.

4 a Cut a 3-ft. (91 cm) piece of beading wire. Center the eighth 15º in the ring from step 1.

b On each end, go through the next existing A and 15º.

c String a color B bicone, a 15º, and a B. Go through the next existing 15º on the color A strand **(photo d)**.

5 On each end, string a B. On one end, string a 15º and string the other end through in the opposite direction **(photo e)**.

6 a On each end, string a B and the next existing 15º on the A strand **(photo f)**.

b Repeat steps 4c–6a until you reach the end of the A strand.

7 Over each pair of strands, string three 15ºs **(photo g)**.

8 On one pair of strands, string a crimp bead. String the other pair through in the opposite direction **(photo h)**.Tighten the wires and crimp the crimp bead. Trim the excess wire.

9 On each end, open a jump ring. Attach half of a toggle clasp. Close the jump ring **(photo i)**.

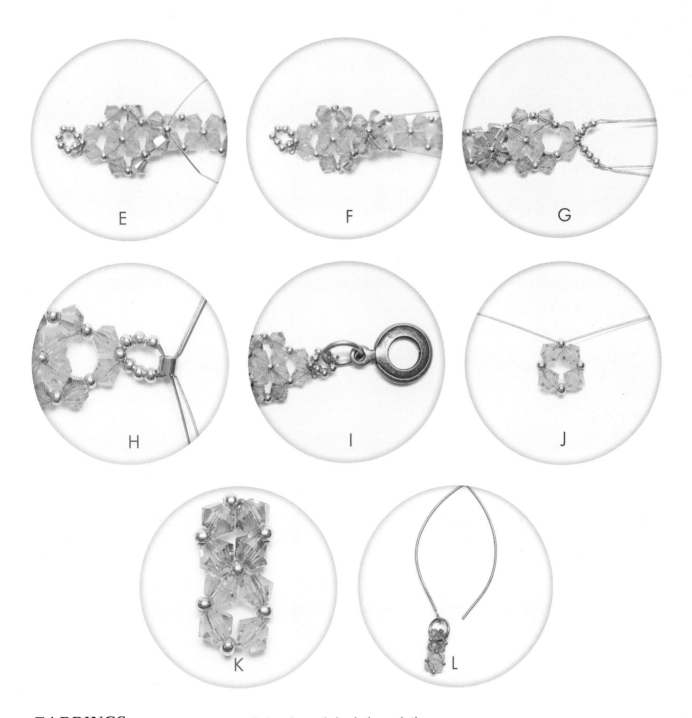

E

F

G

H

I

J

K

L

EARRINGS

1 For each earring: Cut a 6-in. (15cm) piece of beading thread. On the thread, center an alternating patternof four color A bicone crystals and four 15ºs. Tie a surgeon's knot. String one end through the adjacent 15º **(photo j)**.

2 On one end, string a color B bicone, a 15º, and a B. On the other end, string a B, a 15º, a B, and a 15º. Tie a surgeon's knot.

String the ends back through the adjacent beads and trim the excess thread **(photo k)**.

3 Open a jump ring. Attach the dangle and an earring wire. Close the jump ring **(photo l)**.

DOUBLE-THE-FUN WEAVE | Loops of bicones form a lush lattice framework for strands of Charlottes.

● CROSSWEAVE, STRINGING

MATERIALS

- **72–92** 4mm bicone crystals
- hank of charlottes
- flexible beading wire, .014 or .015
- flexible beading wire, .010 or .012
- **2** cones
- **2** crimp beads
- **2** crimp covers
- toggle clasp
- chainnose or crimping pliers
- diagonal wire cutters
- tape or bead stoppers

Color Note The bicones in the copper bracelet are olivine. The bicones in the silver bracelet are Provence lavender AB.

TIP
String the charlottes directly from the hank by inserting the beading wire through the beads, along the hank string, and sliding sections of beads from the string onto the beading wire.

1 a Cut eight 15-in. (38cm) pieces of .010 or .012 beading wire. Cut two 26-in. (66cm) pieces of .014 or .015 beading wire.
b Over all 10 strands, string a crimp bead. Extend the thick wires 4 in. (10cm) from the crimp bead, keeping the fine wires flush with the bead. Crimp the crimp bead **(photo a)**.
2 On each fine wire, string 8–10 in. (20–25cm) of charlottes. Secure the end of each strand with tape or a bead stopper **(photo b)**.
3 On the long end of each thick wire, string: charlotte, bicone crystal, charlotte, bicone, charlotte. String both strands through a bicone in opposite directions **(photo c)**. Repeat until the crystal strand is within 2 in. (5cm) of the finished length. Don't string the strands through a bicone in the last loop.
4 Separate the charlotte strands into two sets of four. String one set

through the second beaded loop. String the other set through the same loop in the opposite direction **(photo d)**.
5 Continue weaving the charlotte strands through the crystal loops. Keep the strands straight and close any gaps between the charlottes **(photo e)**. Don't weave the charlotte strands through the final loop. Add or remove charlottes so all 10 strands are even. Over all 10 strands, string a crimp bead. Tighten the wires and crimp the crimp bead. Trim the fine wires flush with the crimp bead, but leave the thick wires to attach the clasp.
6 On each side, over both thick wires, string a cone, a bicone, a crimp bead, and half of a toggle clasp. Go back through the beads just strung and tighten the wires. Crimp the crimp bead and trim the excess wire **(photo f)**. Close a crimp cover over each crimp.

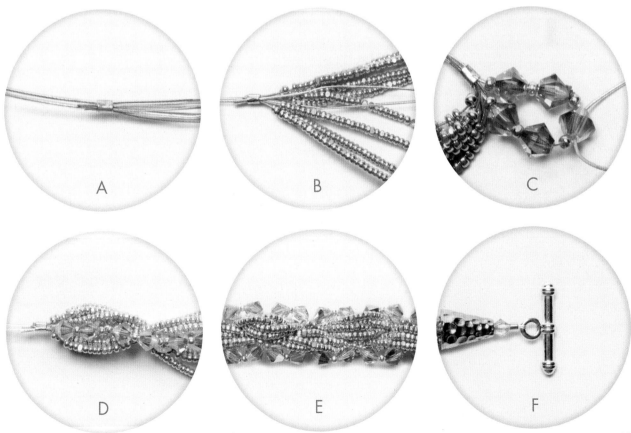

A

B

C

D

E

F

FASHION BOUND

Make tabs from small sections of herringbone stitch to display and evenly space a mix of chains.

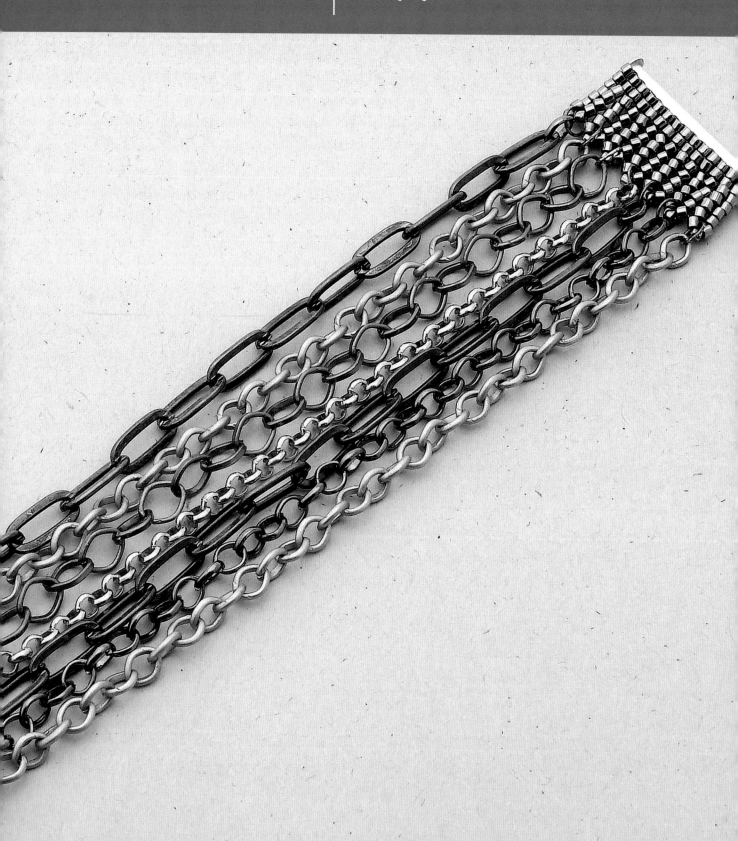

A

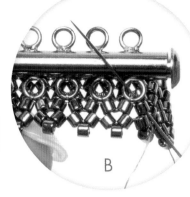

B

C

● HERRINGBONE
MATERIALS
bracelet 7½ in. (19.1cm)

- **7** 6-in. (15cm) pieces of chain in assorted link sizes and finishes
- **5–6** g 10º cylinder beads
- **14** 4–6mm soldered jump rings
- **7**-strand slide clasp
- Fireline 6 lb. test
- beading needles, #12
- **2** pairs of chainnose pliers

1 On 1½ yd. (1.4 m) of Fireline, pick up four 10º cylinder beads, leaving a 15-in. (38cm) tail. Sew through all four cylinders again, stacking the beads into two columns. Working in ladder stitch, pick up two cylinders per stitch to make a strip of bead-work two beads tall and 14 stitches long. Zigzag back through the bead-work so the working thread and tail are exiting opposite ends of the first stitch in the strip.

2 Work a row of flat herringbone stitch using two cylinders per stitch. At the end of the row, make a concealed turn. Repeat for a total of four rows of herringbone stitch.

3 For the next row, pick up two cylinders and a soldered jump ring per stitch, making sure the soldered jump ring sits centered between the two cylinders in each stitch **(photo a)**. After completing the row, sew through all the beads in the end column, then reinforce the beadwork by zigzagging through the remaining columns. Sew through the beadwork to exit the end bead in the last row added.

4 Work the final row using only one cylinder per stitch; then end the working thread.

5 Using the tail, sew through the beadwork to exit a bead in the first herringbone row that corresponds with a clasp loop **(photo b).**

Sew through the loop and the next few beads in the row to exit near the next loop. Repeat to attach all the loops on this half of the clasp, retrace the thread path, and end the tail.

6 Repeat steps 1–5 to make a second beaded tab and attach the other half of the clasp. Make sure the clasp half is positioned so it lines up correctly with the other clasp half.

7 Open an end link on one of the chains as you would a jump ring, and attach it to a soldered jump ring on one of the beaded tabs **(photo c)**. Close the link. Open the link on the other end of the same chain, and attach it to the corresponding soldered jump ring on the other beaded tab. Close the link.

8 Repeat step 7 to attach the remaining chains.

TIP
If your chain has soldered links, sew through the end links of the chains instead of separate soldered jump rings.

DESIGN OPTION
This style also works as a necklace by adjusting the lengths of the chain to drape at any length desired.

TIP
Attach the chain lengths directly to the clasp to omit the stitching in this design.

TWINING VINES

Pair bugle beads and
ladder stitch to create
a vine-like bracelet.

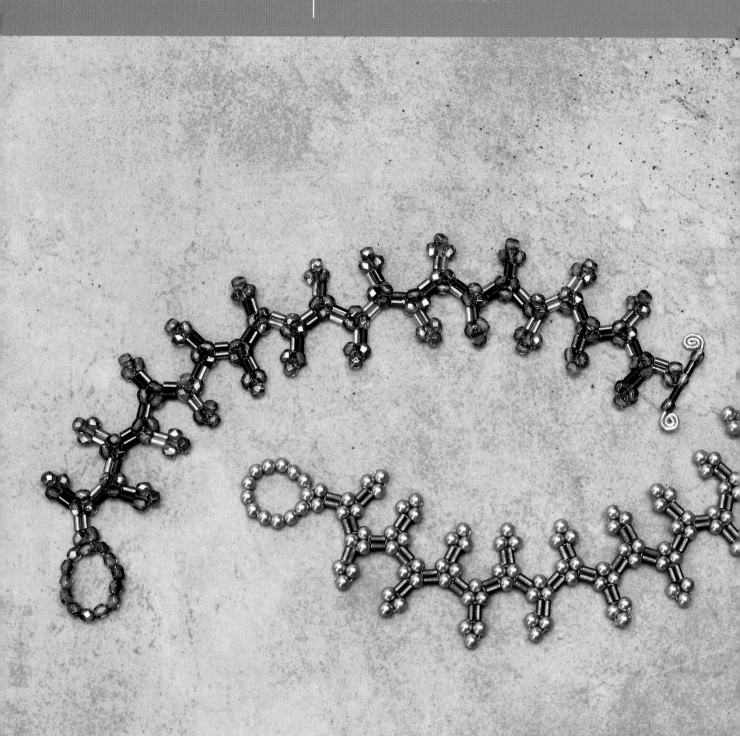

42

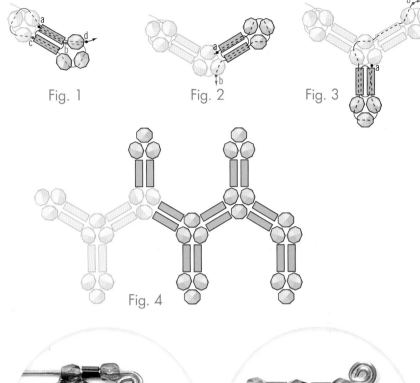

Fig. 1   Fig. 2   Fig. 3

Fig. 4

● LADDER STITCH

MATERIALS
bracelet 7 in. (18cm)

- **150** 3mm Czech fire-polished beads
- 10 g 3mm Japanese bugle beads
- 2 in. (5cm) 22-gauge wire
- Fireline 6 lb. test
- beading needles, #12
- chainnose pliers
- roundnose pliers
- wire cutters

A

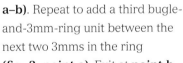

B

C

1 On 3 yd. (2.7m) of Fireline, pick up three 3mm Czech fire-polished beads. Leaving a 12-in. (30cm) tail, tie a surgeon's knot, forming a small ring.

2 Exit the next 3mm in the ring **(fig. 1, point a)**. Pick up two bugle beads, bring both beads up to the ring, and sew through the first bugle **(a–b)**. Pick up three 3mms, and sew through the second bugle **(b–c)**, the three 3mms in the previous ring, the first bugle, and the first 3mm in the new ring **(c–d)**.

3 Add a second bugle-and-3mm-ring unit between the next two 3mms in the ring, and sew through the next 3mm in the ring **(fig. 2,**

a–b). Repeat to add a third bugle-and-3mm-ring unit between the next two 3mms in the ring **(fig. 3, point a)**. Exit at **point b**.

4 Continue stitching, repeating step 3 and referring to **figs. 3** and **4**, until you have a total of 11 bugle-and-3mm-ring units sticking out of each side. Secure the thread in the beadwork with a few half-hitch knots, and trim.

5 With the 12-in. (30cm) tail exiting the end 3mm, use it to pick up 12 3mms. Sew back through the bead your thread is exiting to form a loop **(photo a)**. Retrace the thread path several times to reinforce the loop. Secure the tail, and trim.

6 On 2 in. (5cm) of wire, use the tip of roundnose pliers to make a small loop on one end. Grasp the loop in the chainnose pliers and turn the wire to make a small coil **(photo b)**. String a 3mm and one bugle, and put the wire through the end 3mm **(photo c)**. String one bugle and a 3mm. Make a small coil on the other side of the 3mm.

Ladder stitch in depth

As you work this stitch, the beads begin to resemble the rungs of a ladder—hence the name "ladder stitch." You can use almost any style of bead, or use two or more beads as one in each stitch, which results in a variety of looks that you can use in many ways. Ladder stitch is used most often as a base for brick stitch or herringbone.

The common way to work ladder stitch is to pick up two beads, sew back through the first bead (**fig. 1, a–b**), and then sew through the second bead (**b–c**). Add subsequent beads by picking up one bead, sewing through the previous bead, and then sewing through the new bead (**c–d**).

This is the most common technique, but it produces uneven tension along the ladder of beads because of the alternating pattern of a single thread bridge on the edge between two beads and a double thread bridge on the opposite edge between the same two beads. You can easily correct the uneven tension by zigzagging back through the beads in the opposite direction after you've stitched your ladder to the desired length (**fig. 2**). Doing this creates a double thread path along both edges of the ladder. This aligns the beads right next to each other but fills the bead holes with extra thread, which can cause a problem if you are using small beads.

When you're using ladder stitch to create a base for brick stitch, having the holes filled with thread doesn't matter because rows of brick stitch are worked off the thread bridges, not by sewing through the beads. If you're using the ladder as a base for herringbone, extra thread is potentially problematic, since you're sewing through the ladder base more than once.

Alternate ladder stitch methods

You can use two alternate methods to work ladder stitch, each of which produces beadwork with even tension. The first, a cross-needle technique, results in a single thread path on each edge. To begin, center a bead on the thread. Pick up a bead on one needle and cross the other needle through it (**fig. 3, a–b and b–c**). Add each subsequent bead in the same manner.

To begin the other alternate method, pick up all the beads you need to reach the length your pattern calls for. Sew back through the second-to-last bead in the same direction (**fig. 4, a–b**). Sew through the next bead in the ladder in the same direction (**fig. 5 a–b**). Continue sewing back through each bead until you exit the last bead of the ladder.

Creating a ring

If you'll be working in tubular brick stitch or herringbone stitch, sew your ladder into a ring to provide a base for the new technique. With your thread exiting the last bead in your ladder, sew through the first bead and then back through the last bead, or cross the needles through the first bead if you are using the two-needle technique.

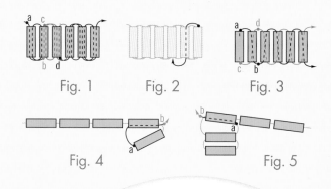

Fig. 1   Fig. 2   Fig. 3

Fig. 4   Fig. 5

The ladder at the bottom has only one bead per stitch, the next has bugle beads, the next has triangle beads, and the top has two beads per stitch.

TACTILE TREASURES

Flat odd-count peyote stitch produces a fantastic band; including different bead shapes and sizes injects texture into the design.

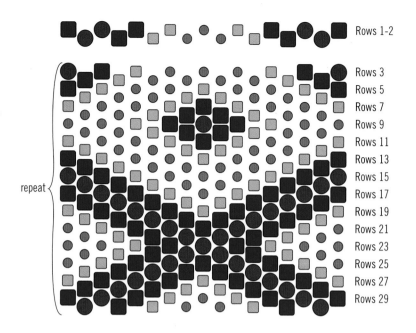

Rows 1-2
Rows 3
Rows 5
Rows 7
Rows 9
Rows 11
Rows 13
Rows 15
Rows 17
Rows 19
Rows 21
Rows 23
Rows 25
Rows 27
Rows 29

repeat

● ODD-COUNT PEYOTE
MATERIALS
burgundy bracelet 7 in. (18cm)

- 2–3 g 11º seed beads, color A (Toho 703, matte mauve mocha)
- 2–3 g 11º cylinder beads, color B (Miyuki 0792, semi-frost opaque shale)
- 2–3 g 15º cylinder beads, color C (Miyuki 0380, matte metallic khaki/pink)
- 3–4 g 15º seed beads, color D (Toho 460A, raspberry bronze iris)
- 2-strand clasp
- Fireline 6 lb. test
- beading needles, #12

green bangle 7-in. (18cm) inner circumference

- 3–4 g 8º seed beads, color A (Miyuki 3205, magic emerald marine-lined crystal)
- 2–3 g 10º cylinder beads, color B (Miyuki 0373, matte metallic sage green luster)
- 2–3 g 11º seed beads, color C
- (Miyuki 459H, emerald green metallic iris)
- 2–3 g 12º three-cut seed beads, color D (953, turquoise-lined jonquil)
- 1–2 g 15º cylinder beads, color E (Miyuki 1053, matte metallic plum green gold iris)
- 1–2 g 15º seed beads, color F (Toho 457, green tea gold luster)
- 1–2 g 15º seed beads, color G (Toho F463B, matte metallic teal iris)
- Fireline 6 lb. test
- beading needles, #12

TIP
As a design option, stitch a band wide enough to fit comfortably around the largest part of your hand, and simply zip up the ends for a bold bangle.

BURGUNDY BRACELET

1 On a comfortable length of Fireline, attach a stop bead, leaving a 20-in (51cm) tail. Work in flat odd-count peyote stitch, referring to chart above:

Rows 1 and 2: Pick up a color B 11º cylinder bead, two color A 11º seed beads, two Bs, two color C 15º cylinder beads, three color D 15º seed beads, two Cs, two Bs, two As, and a B. These beads will shift to form rows 1 and 2 as row 3 is worked.

Row 3: Work eight stitches in flat peyote in the following pattern, picking up one bead per stitch: A, B, C, D, D, D, C, B. Work an odd-count turn with an A.

Row 4: Work eight stitches: B, C, D, D, D, D, C, B.

2 Work as in rows 3 and 4 for rows 5–30, working an odd-count turn at the end of every odd-numbered row.

Row 5: B, C, D, D, C, D, D, C, B.
Row 6: C, D, D, C, C, D, D, C.
Row 7: C, D, D, C, B, C, D, D, C.
Row 8: D, D, C, B, B, C, D, D.
Row 9: D, D, C, B, A, B, C, D, D.
Row 10: D, D, C, B, B, C, D, D.
Row 11: C, D, D, C, B, C, D, D, C.
Row 12: C, D, D, C, C, D, D, C.

Row 13: B, C, D, D, C, D, D, C, B.
Row 14: B, C, D, D, D, D, C, B.
Row 15: A, B, C, D, D, D, C, B, A.
Row 16: A, B, C, D, D, C, B, A.
Row 17: B, A, B, C, D, C, B, A, B.
Row 18: B, A, B, C, C, B, A, B.
Row 19: C, B, A, B, C, B, A, B, C.
Row 20: C, B, A, B, B, A, B, C.
Row 21: D, C, B, A, B, A, B, C, D.
Row 22: D, C, B, A, A, B, C, D.
Row 23: D, D, C, B, A, B, C, D, D.
Row 24: D, C, B, A, A, B, C, D.
Row 25: D, C, B, A, B, A, B, C, D.
Row 26: C, B, A, B, B, A, B, C.
Row 27: C, B, A, B, C, B, A, B, C.
Row 28: B, A, B, C, C, B, A, B.
Row 29: B, A, B, C, D, C, B, A, B.
Row 30: A, B, C, D, D, C, B, A.

3 Repeat rows 3–30 until you are about 1¼ in. (3.2cm) short of the desired length, ending and adding thread as needed.

4 Using the working thread, repeat rows 3–7, replacing the Cs and Bs in the center of rows 6 and 7 with Ds. This will create a smoother end row to connect the clasp.

5 Sew through the end row to exit a bead that lines up with one of the loops of half of the clasp. Pick up seven Ds, and sew through the loop. Skip the last six Ds, and sew back

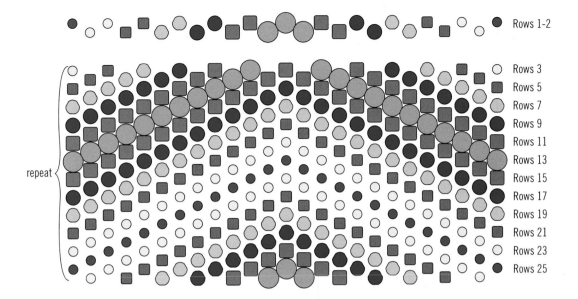

Rows 1-2
Rows 3
Rows 5
Rows 7
Rows 9
Rows 11
Rows 13
Rows 15
Rows 17
Rows 19
Rows 21
Rows 23
Rows 25

repeat

through the first D picked up for a seed bead loop. Sew through the next few beads in the end row to exit near the remaining loop of this half of the clasp. Repeat the seed bead loop, retrace the thread path to secure both seed bead loops, and end the working thread.

6 Using the tail, repeat rows 18–30, and then repeat steps 4 and 5.

GREEN BANGLE

1 On a comfortable length of Fireline, attach a stop bead, leaving a 10-in. (25cm) tail. Work in flat odd-count peyote stitch, referring to chart above:

Rows 1 and 2: Pick up a color G 15º seed bead, two color F 15º seed beads, two color E 15º cylinder beads, two color D 12º three-cut beads, two color C 11º seed beads, two color B 10º cylinder beads, three color A 8ºseed beads, two Bs, two Cs, two Ds, two Es, two Fs, and a G. These beads will shift to form rows 1 and 2 as row 3 is worked.

Row 3: Work 12 stitches in flat peyote in the following pattern, picking up one bead per stitch: F, E, D, C, B, A, B, A, B, C, D, E. Work an odd-count turn with an F.

Row 4: Work 12 stitches: E, D, C, B, A, B, B, A, B, C, D, E.

2 Work rows 3 and 4 as in rows 5–26, working an odd-count turn at the end of every odd-numbered row.

Row 5: E, D, C, B, A, B, C, B, A, B, C, D, E.

Row 6: D, C, B, A, B, C, C, B, A, B, C, D.

Row 7: D, C, B, A, B, C, D, C, B, A, B, C, D.

Row 8: C, B, A, B, C, D, D, C, B, A, B, C.

Row 9: C, B, A, B, C, D, E, D, C, B, A, B, C.

Row 10: B, A, B, C, D, E, E, D, C, B, A, B.

Row 11: B, A, B, C, D, E, F, E, D, C, B, A, B.

Row 12: A, B, C, D, E, F, F, E, D, C, B, A.

Row 13: A, B, C, D, E, F, G, F, E, D, C, B, A.

Row 14: B, C, D, E, F, G, G, F, E, D, C, B.

Row 15: B, C, D, E, F, G, F, G, F, E, D, C, B.

Row 16: C, D, E, F, G, F, F, G, F, E, D, C.

Row 17: C, D, E, F, G, F, E, F, G, F, E, D, C.

Row 18: D, E, F, G, F, E, E, F, G, F, E, D.

Row 19: D, E, F, G, F, E, D, E, F, G, F, E, D.

Row 20: E, F, G, F, E, D, D, E, F, G, F, E.

Row 21: E, F, G, F, E, D, C, D, E, F, G, F, E.

Row 22: F, G, F, E, D, C, C, D, E, F, G, F.

Row 23: F, G, F, E, D, C, B, C, D, E, F, G, F.

Row 24: G, F, E, D, C, B, B, C, D, E, F, G.

Row 25: G, F, E, D, C, B, A, B, C, D, E, F, G.

Row 26: F, E, D, C, B, A, A, B, C, D, E, F.

3 Repeat rows 3–26 until the band fits comfortably around the largest part of your hand. End and add thread as needed.

4 Using the working thread, zip up the first and last rows to form the bangle.

TIP

Use moderate tension throughout the band of beadwork. Ease up on the tension a bit when you switch from a smaller bead to a larger bead, and pull a little tighter when you switch from a larger bead to a smaller bead, to help produce the curvy profile.

CELLINI SAMPLER

Cellini technique is the result of graduating the size of beads in each stitch of flat or tubular peyote stitch.

TIP
The Cellini spiral evolved from a technique taught by seed bead masters Virginia Blakelock and Carol Perrenoud. Virginia developed the tubular stitch, naming it after Benvenuto Cellini, a 16th-century Italian sculptor known for his rococo architectural columns. Somewhere along the line the flat version emerged, and both techniques are truly versatile.

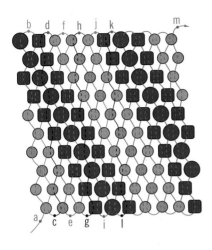

Fig. 1

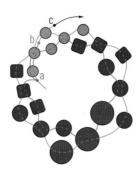

Fig. 2

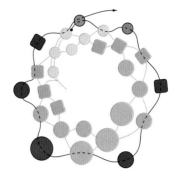

Fig. 3

● CELLINI
MATERIALS

samples

- 1–3 g each of **4** sizes of beads:
- 15º seed beads in each of **2** colors: A, B
- 11º cylinder beads, color C
- 11º seed beads, color D
- 8º seed beads, color E (spiral sample only)
- Fireline 6 lb. test, or nylon beading thread, size D
- beading needles, #12

Materials Note

The look of this technique can vary greatly depending on the size of beads you use. Experiment by stitching small samples until you find your favorite.

FLAT CELLINI SAMPLE

1 On a comfortable length of thread, pick up two color A 15º seed beads, two color B 15º seed beads, two As, two color C 11º cylinder beads, and two color D 11º seed beads (**fig. 1, a–b**). This bead sequence will make up the first two rows of peyote.

2 Working in flat even-count peyote stitch, pick up the following beads, one per stitch:

Row 3: C, D, C, A, B (**b–c**).
Row 4: B, A, C, D, C (**c–d**).
Row 5: A, C, D, C, A (**d–e**).
Row 6: A, C, D, C, A (**e–f**).
Row 7: B, A, C, D, C (**f–g**).
Row 8: C, D, C, A, B (**g–h**).
Row 9: A, B, A, C, D (**h–i**).
Row 10: D, C, A, B, A (**i–j**).
Row 11: C, A, B, A, C (**j–k**).
Row 12: C, A, B, A, C (**k–l**).

3 Work rows 10–3 in reverse (**l–m**). Continue in the established pattern until you reach the desired length.

TIP
Keep tight tension to avoid thread showing between the transition from larger to smaller beads.

CELLINI SPIRAL SAMPLE

1 On a comfortable length of thread, pick up two color A 15º seed beads, two color B 15º seed beads, two color C 11º cylinder beads, two color D 11º seed beads, two color E 8º seed beads, two Ds, and two Cs. Tie the beads into a ring with a square knot, and sew through the first two As again (**fig. 2, a–b**). This bead sequence makes up the first two rounds of peyote.

2 Working in tubular peyote stitch, pick up the following beads, one per stitch: A, B, C, D, E, D, C. Step up through the first A in the new round (**b–c**).

3 Repeat step 2 (**fig. 3**) to the desired length.

TEMPTING TOGGLES

This closure is worthy of your best beadwork. Better yet, let it double as the focal for a simple strand.

● **CELLINI SPIRAL**

MATERIALS

purple toggle ring 1⅜ in. (3.5cm) and toggle bar 1½ in. (3.8cm)

- **138** 3mm drop beads, color D (Toho 452, blue iris)
- 1–2 g 11º cylinder beads, color C (Toho 1506, light purple satin)
- 2–3 g 15º Czech seed beads, color A (Czech, jet)
- 1–2 g 15º seed beads in each of **2** colors: B (silver lined), E (Toho 505, higher metallic dragonfly)
- Fireline 6 lb. test
- beading needles, #12

green toggle ring/bar colors:

- 3mm drop beads, color D (Toho 162F, opaque rainbow frosted khaki)
- 11º seed beads in place of cylinder beads, color C (Miyuki 4221, galvanized light smoky pewter)
- 15º seed beads in place of Czech seed beads, color A (Miyuki 706, matte raku blue/teal iris)
- 15º seed beads, color B (Toho 995, gold-lined rainbow aqua)
- 15º cylinder beads in place of seed beads, color E (Miyuki 0871, matte opaque dark grey AB)

TOGGLE RING

1 On a comfortable length of Fireline, attach a stop bead, leaving a 6-in. (15cm) tail. Pick up four color A 15º Czech seed beads, two color B 15º seed beads, two color C 11º cylinder beads, two color D 3mm drop beads, and two color E 15º seed beads. Sew through the first A picked up to form a ring **(fig. 1)**. The beads in the ring will shift to form the first two rounds as round 3 is added.

2 Work rounds 3 and 4 in tubular peyote stitch :

Round 3: Pick up an A, skip the next A in the ring, and sew through the following A in the ring **(fig. 2, a–b)**. Pick up a B, skip the next A in the ring, and sew through the following B **(b–c)**. Pick up a C, skip the next B in the ring, and sew through the following C **(c–d)**. Pick up a D, skip the next C in the ring, and sew through the following D **(d–e)**. Pick up an E, skip the next D in the ring, and sew through the following E **(e–f)**. Pick up an A, skip the next E in the ring, and sew through the following A to complete the round **(f–g)**. Step up through the first A added in this round **(g–h)**.

Round 4: Pick up a B, and sew

through the next B in the previous round **(fig. 3, a–b)**. Pick up a C, and sew through the next C in the previous round **(b–c)**. Pick up a D, and sew through the next D in the previous round **(c–d)**. Pick up an E, and sew through the next E in the previous round **(d–e)**. Pick up an A, and sew through the next A in the previous round **(e–f)**. Pick up an A, and sew through the next A in the previous round **(f–g)**. Step up through the first B added in this round **(g–h)**. Notice how the step-up shifts with each round, so that you pick up the next bead in the sequence each time you begin a new round, and you step up through that bead after completing the round.

3 Work rounds 5–8 in tubular peyote stitch, picking up one bead per stitch and stepping up after each round:

Round 5: C, D, E, A, A, B.
Round 6: D, E, A, A, B, C.
Round 7: E, A, A, B, C, D.
Round 8: A, A, B, C, D, E.

4 Repeat rounds 3–8, ending and adding thread as needed, until you reach the desired length and the ends easily touch when bending the tube into a ring.

Fig. 1

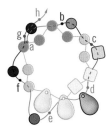

Fig. 2

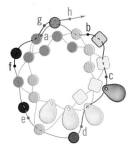

Fig. 3

Fig. 4

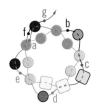

Fig. 5

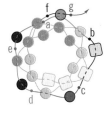

Fig. 6

5 Zip up the end rounds to form a ring. Retrace the thread path of the join, and end the working thread. Remove the stop bead, and end the tail.

TOGGLE BAR

1 On a comfortable length of Fireline, attach a stop bead, leaving a 20-in. (51cm) tail. Pick up four color A 15º Czech seed beads, two color B 15º Seed beads, two color C 11º cylinder beads, and two color E 15º Seed beads. Sew through the first A picked up to form a ring **(fig. 4)**. The beads in the ring will shift to form the first two rounds as round 3 is added.

2 Work rounds 3–7 in tubular peyote stitch.

Round 3: Pick up an A, skip the next A in the ring, and sew through the following A in the ring **(fig. 5, a–b)**. Pick up a B, skip the next A in the ring, and sew through the following B in the ring **(b–c)**. Pick up a C, skip the next B in the ring, and sew through the following C in the ring **(c–d)**. Pick up an E, skip the next C in the ring, and sew through the following E in the ring **(d–e)**. Pick up an A, skip the next E in the ring, and sew through the following

A in the ring to complete the round **(e–f)**. Step up through the first A added in this round **(f–g)**.

Round 4: Pick up a B, and sew through the next B in the previous round **(fig. 6, a–b)**. Pick up a C, and sew through the next C in the previous round **(b–c)**. Pick up an E, and sew through the next E in the previous round **(c–d)**. Pick up an A, and sew through the next A in the previous round (d–e). Pick up an A, and sew through the next A in the previous round **(e–f)**. Step up through the first B added in this round **(f–g)**. Notice how the step-up shifts with each round, so that you pick up the next bead in the sequence each time you begin a new round, and you step up through that bead after completing the round.

3 Work rounds 5–7 in tubular peyote stitch, picking up one bead per stitch and stepping up after each round:

  Round 5: C, E, A, A, B.
  Round 6: E, A, A, B, C.
  Round 7: A, A, B, C, E.

4 Repeat rounds 3–7, ending and adding thread as needed, for a total of 30 rounds or until the bar is about the same length as the inside diameter of the ring.

5 Work an increase round: Pick up beads in this round in the established pattern until you are ready to pick up a C. Pick up two Ds and a C in the space where the C would have gone, and then finish the round in the established pattern. Step up.

6 Work this round in the established pattern, but when you reach the space before the increase stitch, pick up a B, and sew through the first D picked up in the previous round. Pick up a C, skip the second D picked up in the previous round, and sew through the next C. Finish the round in the established pattern, and step up.

7 Work 10 more rounds in the newly established pattern.

8 Work one more round using only As to close up the end of the tube.

9 Remove the stop bead, and work steps 5–7 on the other end of the tube.

10 If you can see the holes of the Ds or there are unsightly gaps between the Ds, embellish the spiral of Ds with As: Using the longer of the two remaining threads, sew through the beadwork to exit the first D in the spiral of Ds, with the thread pointing toward the other end of the tube. Pick up an A, and sew through the next D in the spiral. Repeat, adding an A between all the Ds in the spiral. This will strengthen the toggle bar and add a design element. End the working thread and tail.

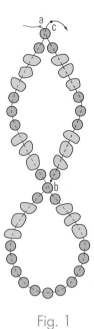

Fig. 1

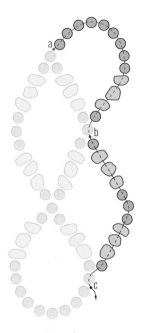

Fig. 2

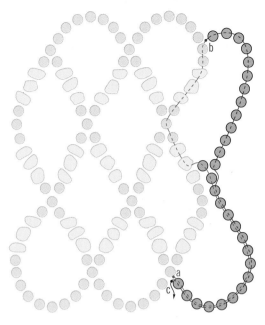

Fig. 3

● NETTING

MATERIALS

bracelet 7 in. (18cm)

- **276** 4mm stone chips
- **4–5 g** 11º seed beads
- clasp
- **2** 4–6mm jump rings
- Fireline 6 lb. test
- beading needles, #12
- **2** pairs of pliers

1 On 3 yd. (2.7 m) of Fireline, attach a stop bead, leaving a 12-in. (30cm) tail. Pick up two 11º seed beads, three stone chips, three 11ºs, three stone chips, three 11ºs, three stone chips, 11 11ºs, three stone chips, and an 11º. Skip the last 19 beads, and sew back through the next 11º **(fig. 1, a–b)**.

2 Pick up an 11º, three stone chips, three 11ºs, three stone chips, and an 11º. Skip 11 beads in the previous row, and sew through the next 11º **(b–c)**.

3 Pick up nine 11ºs, three stone chips, and an 11º. Counting from the 11º your thread exited at the start of this step, skip six beads in the previous row, and sew back through the next 11º **(fig. 2, a–b)**.

4 Pick up an 11º, three stone chips, three 11ºs, three stone chips, and an 11º. Skip 11 beads in the previous row, and sew through the next 11º **(b–c)**.

5 Repeat steps 3 and 4 until the band is about 1 in. (2.5cm) short of the desired length, ending on step 4.

6 Pick up 17 11ºs, skip nine beads in the previous row, and sew through the next stone chip and the next nine beads **(fig. 3, a–b)**. Pick up 13 11ºs, skip the last two 11ºs added in the last stitch, and sew through the next 15 11ºs **(b–c)**. Attach a stop bead to the working thread.

7 Remove the stop bead from the tail, and repeat step 6, but instead of attaching a new stop bead at the end of the step, end the tail.

Q: How do I incorporate a metal clasp into my beaded design?
—*Lisa*

A: There are many choices when it comes to clasps, but really nice clasps usually carry a really nice price tag, so base-metal clasps may be your best alternative. However, slapping an inexpensive metal clasp on a bracelet that took hours to stitch doesn't make sense, and it also diminishes the look of the quality of your work.

Use a beaded clasp to tie in the colors, extend the design of the piece, and give it a more finished look (see "Tempting Toggles" page 50).

If metal is your choice—and sometimes it makes the most sense—consider dressing it with the following ideas:

• Add dangles to a toggle clasp: On a head pin, string a few of the beads used in your beadwork, then make the first half of a wrapped loop. Attach the loop to the toggle ring, and complete the wraps. Repeat to add several dangles, but make sure the toggle bar can still fit through the ring.

You can also use wire to make your own bead-embellished clasps:

• Make a toggle ring with 22–20-gauge wire: Cut about 6 in. (15 cm) of wire, and wrap it around a marker or dowel until the wire crosses. Use one wire end to make a wrapped loop next to the crossed wire. Slide beads on the other wire end until they cover the ring, then wrap the remaining wire over or above the wraps from the wrapped loop. Trim any excess wire.

• To make a toggle bar: Cut about 3 in. (7.6 cm) of wire, and wrap it around a small dowel or roundnose pliers until the wires cross. Twist the wires at the cross once. String several beads on each wire end, and then make a plain loop on each end. Make dangles as described above, open the loop on each end of the toggle bar, and attach the dangles.

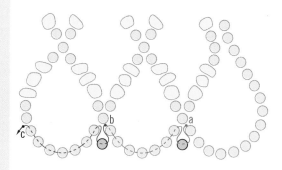

Fig. 4

8 Remove the stop bead from the working thread, pick up an 11º, and sew through the next seven 11ºs along the edge of the bracelet **(fig. 4, a–b)**. Repeat **(b–c)** along the edge until you reach the end. Sew through 28 11ºs on the end of the bracelet, then repeat adding 11ºs along the other edge. Retrace the thread path of the end 11ºs added in step 6, and end the thread.

9 Open a jump ring, and attach half of the clasp around the two center 11ºs on one end of the bracelet **(photo)**. Close the jump ring. Repeat on the other end.

TIP
To use larger stone chips, pick up only two stone chips in each stitch instead of three, and use 8º seed beads instead of 11ºs.

FOUR TIMES THE FUN

Begin with a basic right-angle weave base and then enhance it in three different ways.

MATERIALS

all projects
- Fireline 6 lb. test
- beading needles, #12

single-row bracelet
6½ in. (16.5cm)
- **3** 8mm bicone crystals
- crystal pearls
    - **12** 6mm, color B (dark green)
    - **18** 5mm, color B (dark green)
    - **18** 4mm, color A (light green)
    - **16** 3mm, color A (light green)
- 1–2 g 15º seed beads in each of **2** colors: A, B
- clasp
- **2** 6mm inside-diameter jump rings
- pair of chainnose pliers

double-row bracelet
6½ in. (16.5cm)
- **6** 8mm bicone crystals
- crystal pearls
    - **18** 6mm, color B
    - **30** 5mm, color B
    - **30** 4mm, color A
    - **28** 3mm, color A
- 2–3 g 15º seed beads in each of **2** colors: A, B
- **4** 6mm inside-diameter jump rings
- 2-strand clasp
- pair of chainnose pliers

bangle 2¾ in. (7cm) inner
diameter at widest point
- 8 in. (20cm) circumference
- **12** 8mm bicone crystals
- crystal pearls
    - **24** 6mm, color B
    - **48** 5mm, color B
    - **48** 4mm, color A
    - **36** 3mm, color A
- 4 g 15º seed beads in each of **2** colors: A, B

necklace 18 in. (46cm)
- **24** 8mm bicone crystals
- crystal pearls
    - **48** 6mm, color B
    - **96** 5mm, color B
    - **96** 4mm, color A
    - **81** 3mm, color A
- 5–6 g 15º seed beads in each of **2** colors: A, B
- **2** 6mm inside-diameter jump rings
- clasp
- pair of chainnose pliers

SINGLE-ROW BRACELET

1 On 2 yd. (1.8 m) of Fireline, pick up a repeating pattern of a color A 3mm pearl and a color A 15º seed bead four times, leaving a 12-in (30cm) tail. Sew through the first five beads again to form a ring **(fig. 1, a–b)**.

2 Pick up a repeating pattern of an A 15º and color A 4mm pearl three times, and pick up an A 15º. Working in right-angle weave, sew through the 3mm your thread is exiting and the next four beads **(b–c)**.

3 Continue in right-angle weave: Pick up a repeating pattern of a color B 15º seed bead and a B 5mm pearl three times, pick up a B 15º, and complete the stitch **(c–d)**. Pick up a B 15º, a B 6mm pearl, a B 15º, an 8mm bicone crystal, a B 15º, a B 6mm, and a B 15º, and complete the stitch **(d–e)**. Pick up a B 15º, a B 6mm, a B 15º, a B 5mm, a B 15º, a B 6mm, and a B 15º, and complete the stitch **(e–f)**. Pick up a B 15º, a B 5mm, a B 15º, a B 4mm, a B 15º, a B 5mm, and a B 15º, and complete the stitch **(f–g)**. Pick up an A 15º, a A 4mm, an A 15º, an A 3mm, an A 15º, an A 4mm, and an A 15º, and complete the stitch **(g–h)**. Pick up a repeating pattern of an A 15º and an A 3mm three times, pick up an A 15º, and complete the stitch **(h–i)**.

4 Repeat steps 2 and 3 twice.

5 Retrace the thread path through the last few stitches, tying half-hitch knots between beads. Repeat with the tail, and trim the threads.

6 With a jump ring, attach a clasp half and an end stitch of the beaded strip. Repeat on the other end.

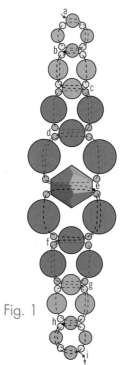

Fig. 1

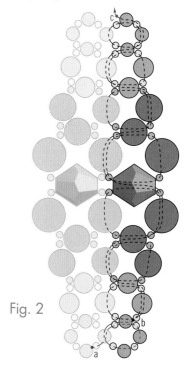

Fig. 2

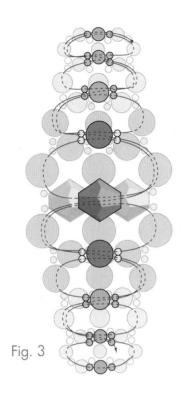

Fig. 3

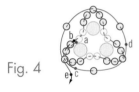

Fig. 4

DOUBLE-ROW BRACELET

1 On 3 yd. (2.7 m) of Fireline, work steps 1–4 of "Single-Row Bracelet," but don't trim the working thread or tail. Sew through an A 15º and an edge A 3mm **(fig. 2, point a)**.

2 Pick up a repeating pattern of an A 15º and A 3mm three times, and pick up an A 15º. Sew through the 3mm your thread is exiting and the next two beads **(a–b)**.

3 Continue working in right-angle weave along the length of the bracelet, picking up the corresponding beads used in each stitch **(b–c)**.

4 Secure the working thread and tail, and trim. Open two jump rings, attach half of the clasp and the end stitches of the strip, and close the jump rings. Repeat on the other end of the bracelet.

BANGLE

1 At the center of a 4-yd. (3.7 m) length of Fireline, work steps 1–3 of "Single-Row Bracelet" four times, but stop before you complete the last strip.

2 Pick up an A 15º, an A 3mm, and an A 15º. Sew through the 3mm from the first stitch, and pick up an A 15º, an A 3mm, and an A 15º. Sew through the 3mm your thread is exiting.

3 Reinforce the join, then exit an edge 3mm. Working in right-angle weave, refer to **fig. 2** to add the second round, then join the first and last stitch as before.

4 Thread a needle on the tail, fold the two rounds together between your finger and thumb, and work the last round of right-angle weave, picking up the corresponding beads in each stitch **(fig. 3)**.

5 Secure the working thread and tail, and trim.

NECKLACE

1 Ending and adding thread as needed, work steps 1–3 of "Single-Row Bracelet" eight times.

2 Refer to **fig. 2** to add the second row of right- angle weave.

3 Fold the two rows between your finger and thumb, and work a third row of right-angle weave, picking up the corresponding beads in each stitch **(fig. 3)**.

4 To finish the ends, exit an A 15º to the left of an A 3mm. Pick up five A 15ºs, and sew down through the A 15º to the right of the same 3mm. Sew up through the next A 15º. Repeat twice to add A 15ºs above the other two 3mms **(fig. 4, a–b)**.

5 Sew through the first three A 15ºs added in the previous step **(b–c)**. Pick up an A 15º, and sew through the third A 15º in the next set of five A 15ºs **(c–d)**. Repeat twice to form the A 15ºs into a tight ring **(d–e)**.

6 With a jump ring, attach a clasp half. Repeat with the other half of the clasp.

7 Pick up an A 3mm, 13 A 15ºs, and the jump ring of one half of the clasp. Sew back through the 3mm, enclosing the jump ring in the loop. Continue through the A 15º opposite the A 15º your thread exited at the start of this step. Retrace the thread path to reinforce the loop, secure the working thread and tail, and trim.

8 Repeat steps 4–7 on the other end of the necklace.

URBAN ARMOR

Peanut beads plus right-angle weave produce a thick beadwork band. Embedded crystals and pearls add subtle glamour.

● RIGHT-ANGLE WEAVE

MATERIALS
bracelet 7 in. (18cm)

- 17.5 g 2x4mm peanut beads (P4018, matte pebble)
- **112** 3mm round pearls in each of **2** colors: A (Swarovski, jet black), B (Swarovski, dark gray)
- **56** 3mm round crystals, color C (Swarovski, greige)
- 5-strand slide clasp
- **10** 6mm jump rings
- Fireline 6 lb. test

TIP
To keep track of your place as you repeat steps 3 and 4, remember this: If you are exiting a peanut bead, pick up an accent bead first, and if you are exiting an accent bead, pick up a peanut bead first.

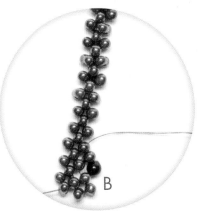

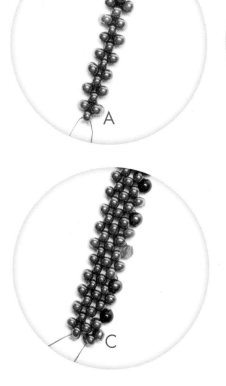

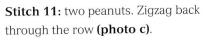

1 On a comfortable length of Fireline, pick up four 2x4mm peanut beads, leaving a 6-in. (15cm) tail. Tie the beads into a ring with a square knot.

2 Work a strip of 11 stitches in right-angle weave using peanut beads. Zigzag back through the strip **(photo a)**.

3 Sew through the last stitch to exit a side peanut bead. Working in right-angle weave, add a row using three peanut beads for the first stitch, and two beads per stitch to complete the row as follows:

Stitch 2: a color A 3mm pearl and a peanut **(photo b)**.

Stitch 3: two peanuts.

Stitch 4: a color B 3mm pearl and a peanut.

Stitch 5: two peanuts.

Stitch 6: a color C round crystal and a peanut.

Stitch 7: two peanuts.

Stitch 8: a B and a peanut.

Stitch 9: two peanuts.

Stitch 10: an A and a peanut.

Stitch 11: two peanuts. Zigzag back through the row **(photo c)**.

4 Add a row as in step 3, but in the stitches with 3mm accent beads, pick up a peanut bead first then the accent bead.

5 Repeat steps 3 and 4 to the desired length, ending and adding thread as needed.

6 Work the last row using all peanut beads. End the working thread and tail.

7 Open a 6mm jump ring, and attach an end stitch and a loop of half of the clasp **(photo d)**. Close the jump ring. Repeat to attach the remaining loops of this half of the clasp. Attach the other half of the clasp on the other end of the bracelet.

TIP
Zigzagging back through the rows may seem like a waste of time, but this reinforces the rows as you work, making a sturdier bracelet. It also helps to maintain even tension throughout the piece.

DESIGN OPTION
Think thin. Make narrow cuffs three stitches wide, using peanut beads for the edge stitches and an accent bead and a peanut bead for the center stitch. Join the end stitches to make a bangle, or attach a single-loop clasp as for the wide cuff.

VICTORIAN INSPIRATION

Tiny gemstones and seed beads mimic the intricate, feminine style of the Victorian era in modified right-angle weave earrings.

● PICOT TECHNIQUE
MATERIALS
earrings

- **88** 3mm faceted round garnet beads
- 1 g 15º seed beads
- pair of earring findings
- Fireline 4 lb. test, smoke color
- beading needles, #13
- **2** pairs of chainnose pliers

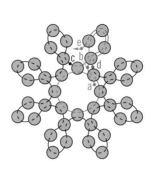

Fig. 1

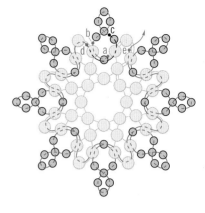

Fig. 2

1 On 2 yd. (1.8 m) of Fireline, leaving a 6-in. (15cm) tail, pick up eight 3mm garnet beads. Sew back through the first 3mm to form a ring **(fig. 1, a–b)**.

2 Pick up four 3mms, skip the last three, and sew back through the first 3mm and the next 3mm in the ring **(b–c)**, making the first picot. Repeat seven times to make a total of eight picots. Sew through the first 3mm in the ring **(c–d)** and on through four 3mms in the first picot **(d–e)**.

3 Pick up one 15º seed bead, and sew through the side 3mm in the next picot **(fig. 2, a–b)**. Pick up five 15ºs, and sew through the second 15º in the same direction **(b–c)**. Pick up a 15º, and sew through the side 3mm from the previous picot, the 15º, and the side 3mm in the next picot **(c–d)**. Sew through the next two beads.

4 Repeat step 3 seven times **(d–e)**.

5 Sew through the next two 3mms, a 15º, a 3mm from the next picot, and four 15ºs as shown **(fig. 3, a–b)**. Pick up a 3mm, a 15º, a 3mm, and seven 15ºs. Sew through the first 15º of the seven to form a ring **(b–c)**. Pick up a 3mm, a 15º, and a 3mm. Sew back through four 15ºs and a side 3mm as shown **(c–d)**.

6 Secure the working thread with a few half-hitch knots, and trim. Repeat with the tail.

7 Open the loop of an earring finding, and attach the loop of 15ºs.

8 Make a second earring.

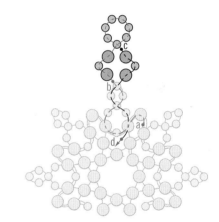

Fig. 3

TIP
I made a smaller version of these earrings by only making four picots in step 2. Then I added 15º seed beads between those picots, as in step 3, and added one 15º between the remaining 3mms in the ring. I added a small loop of seven 15ºs to the top 3mm in the ring for the earring finding.

ASKANNA

Q: What's the best way to control tension as I am beading?
–Jennifer

A: Here's a list of the most common tension problems and my solutions. Do any of them sound familiar?

1. Picking up your beadwork can greatly improve your stitching tension. Holding the beads in the stitch you just added and the working thread where it exits the last bead will prevent the stitch from loosening up as you add the next stitch. Only let go of the working thread once the next stitch is completed, and then only to move your grasp down to the next stitch.

2. Don't skimp on stitching, reinforcing, or ending and adding thread. Take the time to reinforce a row or round if it is loose or uneven; otherwise, all your time is wasted. Work with manageable lengths of thread—about 2 yd. (1.8 m). If you are determined to work with double that length or more, work from the middle of the thread and wrap the remainder of the thread on a bobbin or piece of cardboard.

3. To create even tension for right-angle weave (RAW) stitches, reinforce each row or round once it is completed instead of only reinforcing each stitch. The RAW thread path produces two threads on one side of each stitch and one thread on the other. No matter how many times you retrace the stitch, there will still be more thread paths on one side than the other. Only zigzagging back through the row (or round) will correct this.

4. To create good tension as you start a strip of flat even-count peyote stitch, work a row as usual, but when the working thread and tail are on the same side of the beadwork, place your thumbnail next to the edge beads and slide it up toward the beads as you pull the working thread and tail in the opposite direction. This will snug up the beads in the first three rows, and as you repeat this for the next several pairs of rows, you will start out with tight, even tension. For flat odd-count peyote stitch, snug up the beadwork as described, but do so before adding the last bead in the odd-count turn row. For even- or odd-count stitches, once you get past the first several rows, only pull on the working thread as you snug up the row just completed; the tail will no longer help as you continue working.

5. When working with any stitch in the round, begin the first few rows around a dowel or pencil. Once you get those first rounds done, it should be easier to maintain even stitches.

6. Working with doubled thread fills the bead holes, resulting in better tension. It can be a pain, though, if it knots or if you have to remove stitches. Work with doubled thread only if you already have command of the stitch. For similar results, stick with a single, but thicker, thread. If the project calls for 6 lb. Fireline, try using 8 lb. Working with a thicker thread usually means working with a needle with a larger eye, so make sure that the holes in the beads will accommodate the needle and thread.

7. Working with the correct thread will improve your tension by providing the proper strength for the beads you are using. If you are using beads that may have sharp edges along the holes, such as crystals or bugle beads, use a strong fray-resistant thread like Fireline, Power Pro, or WildFire. These threads were adopted from sport fishing. They resist breaking so you don't have to be as cautious as you would with a nylon thread. You'll get a feel for how hard you can pull with each type of bead by keeping track of how and when you break thread as you work.

8. Conditioning thread with either microcrystalline or beeswax adds a tacky coating, allowing the thread to stick to itself. Waxed thread holds each stitch in place better than unconditioned thread. Also, if you use doubled thread, waxing the strands together will help them act as a single thread and reduce tangles or knots.

9. Some stitches work better with certain beads. If you are having a difficult time maintaining tension with a certain stitch, try out another type or size bead before abandoning it all together. For example, if you are working on a strip of herringbone stitch and you just can't get the stitches to lay the way you want, try using a smaller bead. Oftentimes, smaller beads nestle next to each other better and disguise the thread path that can be very apparent in herringbone pieces.

FIT FOR A QUEEN

Seed bead bases, embellished on both sides, give modified right-angle weave the look and feel of jewels.

MATERIALS

necklace 16 in. (41cm)

- Swarovski crystals
    - **3** 16x11mm pendants
    - **124** 4mm bicones
    - **108** 3mm bicones
- seed beads
    - 15 g 8º
    - 20 g 11º
    - 15 g 5º
- clasp
- **2** 8mm jump rings
- Fireline 6 lb. test
- beading needles, #12
- **2** pair of chainnose pliers

This design is fairly formal. Omit the dangles for a more casual version of this necklace or a matching bracelet.

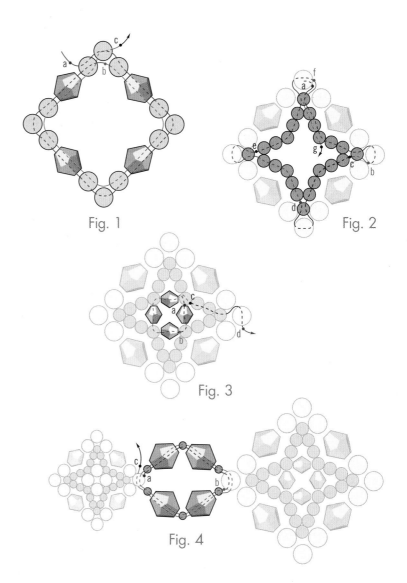

Fig. 1

Fig. 2

Fig. 3

Fig. 4

LARGE UNITS

1 On 3 yd. (2.7 m) of Fireline, pick up a repeating pattern of three 8º seed beads and a 4mm bicone crystal four times, leaving a 10-in. (25cm) tail. Sew through the first 8º again **(fig. 1, a–b)**. Retrace the thread path, skipping the center 8º in each set of three, and pulling tightly to bring the beads into a diamond shape. Exit the center 8º of the first set **(b–c)**.

2 Pick up seven 11º seed beads, sew through the next center 8º **(fig. 2, a–b)**, and sew back through the seventh 11º **(b–c)**.

3 Pick up six 11ºs, sew through the next center 8º, and sew back through the sixth 8º **(c–d)**. Repeat **(d–e)**.

4 Pick up five 11ºs, and sew through the first 11º from step 2 and the next center 8º **(e–f)**. Sew through the first four 11ºs again **(f–g)**.

5 Pick up a 3mm bicone crystal, skip five 11ºs, and sew through the next 11º **(fig. 3, a–b)**. Repeat three times **(b–c)**. Retrace the center thread path to reinforce the crystals added in this step. Sew through the beadwork to exit a center 8º **(c–d)**.

6 Flip the beadwork, and repeat steps 2–5 on the other side. Don't trim the working threads or tails, as they will be used to connect the units.

7 Repeat steps 1–6 to make a total of nine large units.

SMALL UNITS

Make nine small units by repeating steps 1–7 of "Large Units," but substitute 3mms for the 4mms, 11ºs for 8ºs, and 15º seed beads for 11ºs.

CRYSTAL CONNECTIONS

1 Starting with a small unit, thread a needle on one of the tails, making sure the thread is exiting a center 11º **(fig. 4, point a)**.

2 Pick up a 15º, a 4mm, a 15º, a 4mm, and a 15º. Sew through a center 8º on a large unit **(a–b)**, and pick up a 15º, a 4mm, a 15º, a 4mm, and a 15º. Sew back through the 11º your thread exited in the small unit. Retrace the thread path to reinforce the join **(b–c)**. Secure the working thread with a few half-hitch knots, and trim. Don't secure the tail, as you will use it to attach the clasp.

3 Repeat steps 1 and 2, connecting an alternating pattern of small and large units, ending with a small unit. Reserve one large unit for the center dangle.

4 Secure a new thread in the small unit at the middle of the necklace, and exit the center 11º at the bottom of it **(fig. 5, point a)**.

5 Connect the remaining large unit as in steps 1 and 2, but don't secure or trim the thread **(a–b)**. Sew through the beads of the large unit as shown, and exit the opposite 8º **(b–c)**.

6 To add the crystal dangle, pick up a 15º, a 4mm, a 15º, a 4mm, 13 15ºs, and a crystal pendant. Sew through the first 15º of the 13 you just picked up **(c–d)**. Pick up a 4mm, a 15º, a 4mm, and a 15º, and sew back through the 8º your thread exited at the start of this step and the following 15º **(d–e)**. Retrace the thread path, secure the working thread, and trim.

7 Repeat step 6 to add dangles to the two large units on either side of the small center unit.

8 Make a crystal ring on one end of the necklace using the tail from the small unit. With the thread exiting the end center 11º, pick up a 15º, a 4mm, a 15º, a 4mm, a 15º, a 4mm, a 15º, a 4mm, and a 15º. Sew through the end 11º **(fig. 6, a–b),** and retrace the thread path several times to reinforce the ring.

Fig. 6

Fig. 5

Secure the tail, and trim. Repeat on the other end of the necklace.

9 Open a jump ring, and attach half of the clasp to the crystal ring on one end of the necklace. Close the jump ring. Repeat on the other end of the necklace with the other half of the clasp.

DYNAMIC DIAMONDS

Connect one simple stitch in several clever ways for an array of designs.

66

MATERIALS

straight bracelet 8 in. (20cm)
- **6** 4mm pearls (Swarovski, mauve)
- 1–2 g 11º seed beads (Toho 711, nickel-plated silver)
- clasp
- **2** 4mm jump rings
- Fireline 6 lb. test
- beading needles, #12
- **2** pairs of pliers

open pendant colors:
- 2x4mm disk beads (Czech, jet Picasso)
- 11º seed beads (Toho F297, transparent gray matte AB)

embellished pendant colors:
- 4x3mm rondelles (Thunder Polish glass, black/bronze and gray)
- 11º seed beads (Toho 711, nickel-plated silver)

zigzag bracelet colors:
- 4x3mm rondelles (Thunder Polish glass, gray)
- 11º seed beads (Miyuki 2012, matte metallic tawny gray)

Hattie Newman inspired this design in her *Arabesque Pendant*.

TIP
Use two different sizes of any bead combination for greater interest.

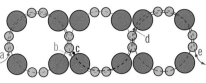

Fig. 1

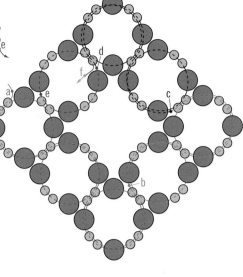

Fig. 2

STRIP OF STITCHES

1 On a comfortable length of Fireline, pick up a repeating pattern of two 11º seed beads and a 4mm pearl four times, leaving a 6-in. (15cm) tail. Sew through all the beads again to form a ring, and exit a pair of 11ºs opposite the tail **(fig. 1, a–b)**.

2 Pick up a repeating pattern of a 4mm and two 11ºs three times, and then pick up a 4mm. Sew through the pair of 11ºs your thread exited at the start of this step **(b–c)**, and continue through the next six beads to exit the pair of 11ºs opposite the join **(c–d)**.

3 Repeat step 2 **(d–e)** for the desired length, ending and adding thread as needed.

DIAMOND COMPONENT

1 Make a strip of three stitches as in "Strip of Stitches." In the third stitch, continue through the next three beads to exit a pair of 11ºs adjacent to the last join **(fig. 2, a–b)**.

2 Work two stitches as in step 2 of "Strip of Stitches," and then sew through the next three beads to exit the pair of 11ºs adjacent to the last join **(b–c)**. Repeat this step **(c–d)**.

3 To join the end stitches, creating the diamond shape, pick up a 4mm, two 11ºs, and a 4mm. Sew through the corresponding pair of 11ºs from the first stitch **(d–e)**. Pick up a 4mm, two 11ºs, and a 4mm, and sew through the pair of 11ºs your thread exited at the start of this step **(e–f)**. Retrace the thread path of the join. To embellish the center of the diamond component, go to step 4; otherwise end the threads.

Q: How do you come up with designs for beaded jewelry? —Linda

A: Most of the time when I sit down to create a new pattern, or incorporate a cool new style of bead into a design, the act of just working with the materials ends up resulting in some sort of jewelry. Not right away, but if I work long enough, something usually begins to emerge. If I feel like I am "blocked," I just keep going. A lot of the time, I just cut off whatever it was that I was working on, let it go, and start fresh. Sometimes a little part of a stitch, or the way two different beads sit together, is enough to spark a new direction.

But if that doesn't come easy, here are some other ideas:

• Surround yourself with inspiring materials. Fill your work surface with materials you love, but mix it up once and a while.

• If you like a certain designer, or a particular style of jewelry, start there. Make something designed by someone else, then try modifying it as much as possible.

• Learn the basic stitches. I feel like the best thing I did while teaching myself to bead was to learn all of the stitches thoroughly. This way, I could combine the stitches together, making some really interesting designs. See more tips on page 91.

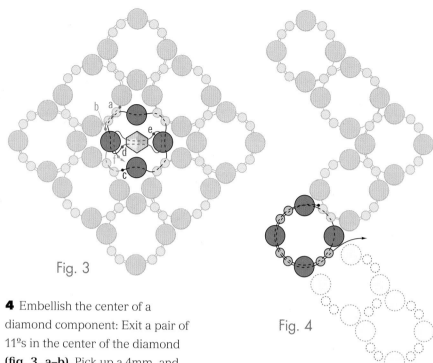

Fig. 3

Fig. 4

4 Embellish the center of a diamond component: Exit a pair of 11ºs in the center of the diamond **(fig. 3, a–b)**. Pick up a 4mm, and sew through the next pair of center 11ºs **(b–c)**. Repeat this stitch around the center of the component, exiting a 4mm **(c–d)**. Pick up a 3–4mm accent bead, and sew through the 4mm opposite the 4mm your thread exited at the start of this stitch **(d–e)**. Sew back through the 3–4mm bead and through the 4mm your thread exited at the start of this stitch **(e–f)**. End the threads.

ZIGZAG

1 Work as in steps 1 and 2 of "Diamond Component," but after the fifth stitch, sew through the beadwork so you will be working away from the first stitch in the beadwork, creating a zigzag instead of a diamond **(fig. 4)**.

2 Continue in this manner to the desired length.

FINISHING OPTIONS
To make a bracelet or necklace, make a loop of seed beads on each end of a strip or zigzag. Open two jump rings, and attach each loop of seed beads to half of the clasp. To make a pendant, make a loop of seed beads at the top of a single diamond component, and use a jump ring to attach the pendant to a chain or other stringing material. For an earring, attach the diamond component to an earring finding. You can also use an open diamond component as a toggle ring.

STANDING OVATION

Combine several bead styles to take the guesswork out of this daring cubic right-angle weave design.

● CUBIC RIGHT-ANGLE WEAVE
MATERIALS

topaz AB bangle inner diameter 7⅜ in. (19cm)

- **144** 4mm bicone crystals (Swarovski, topaz AB)
- **144** 3mm crystal pearls (Swarovski, deep brown)
- **48** 6mm two-hole tile beads (Czech, opaque yellow Picasso)
- 3–4 g 10º cylinder beads (Miyuki DBM0254, bronze luster)
- 2–3 g 11º seed beads (Miyuki 9361, yellow-lined aqua AB)
- 2–3 g 15º seed beads (Miyuki 458, metallic brown iris)
- Fireline 6 lb. test
- beading needles, #12

light gray opal AB bangle colors:

- 4mm bicone crystals (Swarovski, topaz AB 2x)
- 3mm crystal pearls (Swarovski, light green)
- 5mm Tila beads (Miyuki 462, metallic gold iris)
- 10º cylinder beads (Miyuki 0254, bronze luster)
- 11º seed beads (Miyuki 462D, gold iris)
- 11º cylinder beads, substituted for 15º seed beads (Miyuki 029, metallic purple gold iris)

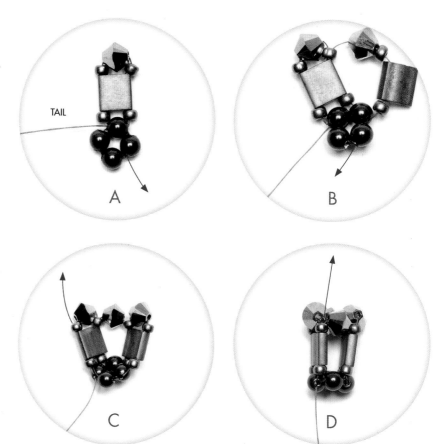

1 On a comfortable length of Fireline, pick up four 3mm pearls, leaving a 6-in. (15cm) tail. Sew through all the pearls again to form a ring, and sew through the first pearl once more so the working thread and tail are exiting opposite ends of the first pearl.

2 Make a spoke: Pick up an 11º seed bead, sew through one hole of a 6mm two-hole tile bead or a 5mm Tila bead, and pick up an 11º, a 4mm bicone crystal, and an 11º. Sew down through the remaining hole of the same tile bead, pick up an 11º, and sew through the pearl your thread exited at the start of this step and the next pearl in the ring **(photo a)**.

3 Pick up an 11º, sew through one hole of a new tile bead, and pick up an 11º and a 4mm. Sew down through the adjacent 11º, tile bead,

and 11º in the previous spoke, and then sew through the pearl your thread exited at the start of this step and the following pearl in the ring **(photo b)**.

4 Pick up an 11º, sew up through the remaining hole of the tile bead just added, and pick up an 11º and a 4mm. Sew down through the 11º, the corresponding hole of the same tile bead, and the next 11º in the new spoke, and then sew through the pearl your thread exited at the start of this step and the following pearl in the ring. Sew up through the nearest 11º, tile bead, and 11º in the previous spoke **(photo c)**.

5 Pick up a 4mm, and sew down through the adjacent 11º, tile bead, and 11º in the previous spoke. Retrace the thread path through the next four beads **(photo d)**.

6 Sew through the ring of 4mms to complete the first cubic right-angle

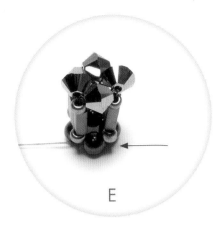

E

F

TIP
- If you are concerned about sizing your bangle or would like to add a clasp to the end units, skip steps 10 and 11 until you've completed the remaining steps. Then, go back to steps 10 and 11 to join the end stitches, or make a seed bead ring on each end to attach a clasp.

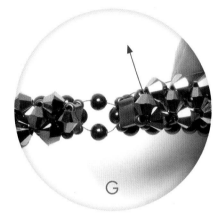

G

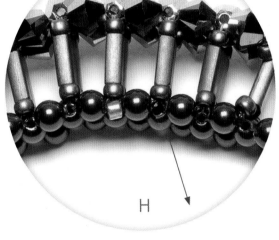

H

weave unit. Sew through the beads in the new spoke, and exit the pearl opposite the one your tail is exiting **(photo e)**.

7 Pick up three pearls, and sew through the pearl your thread exited at the start of this step and the next pearl in the new ring **(photo f)**.

8 Repeat steps 3–7 until you reach the desired length, ending and adding thread as needed. The beadwork must fit around the widest part of your hand minus the length of one stitch. Depending on your stitching tension, the beadwork may snug up a bit in step 12. To avoid making the bangle too small, work one extra stitch if you usually have loose stitching tension.

9 Repeat steps 3–6.

10 Pick up a pearl, and sew through the end pearl of the first pearl ring. Pick up a pearl, and sew through the end pearl of the last pearl ring **(photo g)**. Retrace the thread path to secure the join, and sew up through an 11º, tile bead, and 11º in the last spoke added.

11 Pick up a 4mm, and sew through the 11º, tile bead, and 11º in the first spoke. Retrace the thread path, and sew through the beadwork to add the last 4mm to the top of the bangle. Retrace the thread

path, and end the working thread and tail.

12 Add 2 yd. (1.8 m) of Fireline to the base layer of pearls, exiting an edge pearl on one side of the bangle. Pick up a 15º seed bead, and sew through the next pearl along this edge **(photo h)**. Repeat to complete the round. Sew through the beadwork to exit an edge pearl on the other side of the bangle, and repeat to add a 15º between all the pearls along this edge. End the threads. Repeat this step to add a 10º cylinder between all the 4mms along each outside edge of the bangle.

TIP
I've made two other variations of this bangle using seed beads instead of pearls: 11º seed beads in one and 10º cylinder beads in another. This brought the units closer together, which prompted me to use 3mm bicone crystals in place of the 4mms. If you substitute beads, you may need more tile beads and crystals.

Hang a fused-glass pendant from a chain of seed beads in coordinating colors.

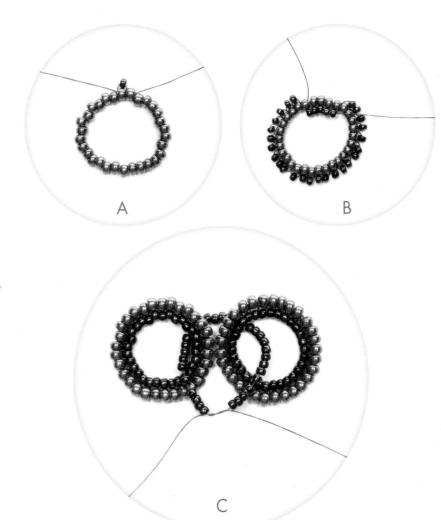

A

B

C

● MODIFIED SQUARE STITCH

MATERIALS

necklace 17 in. (43cm)

- 1¼ x1¹⁄₁₆-in. (3.2x2.7cm) fused-glass pendant (James Daschbach, lilyrosebeads.com)
- 5–8 g 11º seed beads
- 4–7 g 15º seed beads
- clasp
- Fireline 6 lb. test, or nylon beading thread, size D
- beading needles, #12

1 On 1 yd. (.9 m) of Fireline or thread, pick up 30 11º seed beads, leaving a 4-in. (10cm) tail. Sew through all the beads again, and continue through the first 11º. Gently pull the beads into a ring.

2 Pick up a 15º seed bead, and sew through the 11º your thread exited at the start of this step and the next 11º in the ring **(photo a)**. Repeat until you've added a 15º to each 11º in the ring.

3 Sew through the first five 15ºs added. Pull gently to bring the 15ºs to the center of the ring of 11ºs **(photo b)**. Sew through the next few 15ºs, and pull. Continue in this manner, and retrace the thread path through the 15ºs.

4 Sew through the ring of 11ºs to exit next to the tail, and tie the threads together with a square knot.

Sew through the next few 11ºs, and pull the knot into the adjacent 11º. Trim the working thread and tail.

5 Repeat steps 1–4 to make the desired number of links.

6 To connect the links, pick up 30 15ºs on 12 in. (30cm) of thread. Sew through two links, and tie a square knot to form the beads into a ring **(photo c)**. Retrace the thread path several times, and end the threads.

7 Connect the pendant to the center link and the clasp halves to each end link as in step 6, but adjust the number of 15ºs picked up to accommodate the pendant and clasp.

TIP

For an alternate way to make the rings, add a 15º between each pair of 15ºs added in step 2. Instead of pulling the 15ºs to the center of the ring, they will form an outer ring.

POINT OF CONNECTION

Bicone crystals play peek-a-boo, letting square crystal components take center stage.

TIP
For the large component in the pendant and earrings, I used a 6mm bicone in place of the four 4mms, working as for the small component. I used Swarovski amethyst 6mm crystals for the earrings and pendant.

● BEADWEAVING

MATERIALS

three linked components 3½ in. (8.9cm)

- 20mm large crystal square (Swarovski, Bermuda blue)
- **2** 14mm small crystal squares (Swarovski, Bermuda blue)
- **6** 4mm bicone crystals (Swarovski, light tanzanite)
- 1 g 11º seed beads (Miyuki 378, light olive-lined crystal luster)
- 2–3 g 15º seed beads color A (Miyuki 1884, violet gold luster), color B (Toho 457, gold lustered green tea)
- Fireline 6 lb. test
- beading needles, #12

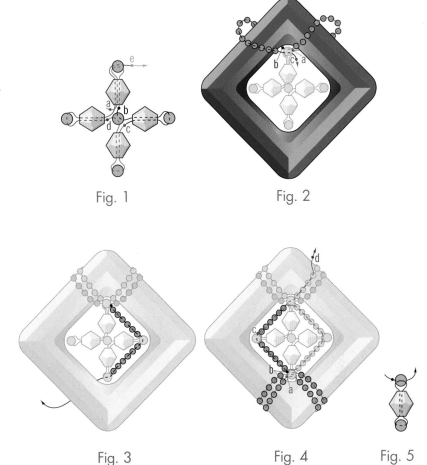

Fig. 1

Fig. 2

Fig. 3

Fig. 4

Fig. 5

LARGE COMPONENT

1 On 1½ yd. (1.4 m) of Fireline, pick up a 4mm bicone crystal and an 11º seed bead, leaving a 12-in. (30cm) tail. Skip the 11º, and sew back through the 4mm **(fig. 1, a–b)**.

2 Pick up an 11º, a 4mm, and an 11º. Skip the last 11º picked up, and sew back through the last 4mm **(b–c)**.

3 Pick up a 4mm and an 11º, skip the last 11º, sew back through the last 4mm, and then sew through the center 11º **(c–d)**.

4 Pick up a 4mm and an 11º, skip the last 11º, sew back through the last 4mm, and then sew through the first 4mm and 11º picked up in step 1 **(d–e)**.

5 Pick up 19 color A 15º seed beads, wrap the beads around one side of one corner of a large crystal square, and sew back through the 11º your thread exited at the start of this step **(fig. 2, a–b)**. Repeat to add a loop of beads around the other side of the same corner **(b–c)**. Retrace the thread path through both loops, exiting the 11º.

6 Repeat step 5 on the same corner, but use color B 15º seed beads, and position the loops to sit under the loops of As.

7 Working on the back side of the component, pick up six As, and sew through the 11º at the end of the next 4mm. Repeat to exit the 11º opposite the one your thread exited at the start of this step **(fig. 3)**, and then repeat steps 5 and 6 on the opposite corner of the large crystal square **(fig. 4, a–b)**. Pick up six As, and sew through the 11º at the end of the next 4mm **(b–c)**. Pick up six As, and sew through all four sets of six As, skipping the end 11ºs. This will make a tight frame around the center bicone embellishment. Sew through the 11º connecting the first set of loops, and then continue through the first four As of one of the loops on the back of the component **(c–d)**.

8 Using the tail, sew through the beadwork to exit the corresponding As on the opposite end of the square, so the working thread exits a loop of As on one end of the square and the tail exits a loop of As on the other end. Don't end the working thread or tail; these threads are used to connect bails or links later.

SMALL COMPONENT

1 On 1 yd. (.9 m) of Fireline, pick up an 11º, a 4mm, and an 11º, leaving a 12-in. (30cm) tail. Skip the last 11º, and sew back through the 4mm and the first 11º so the working thread and tail are exiting opposite ends of the same bead **(fig. 5)**.

2 Pick up 13 As, wrap the beads around one side of one corner of a small crystal square, and sew back through the 11º your thread exited at the start of this step. Repeat to add a loop to the other side of the

Fig. 6

Fig. 7

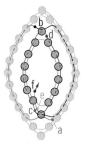

Fig. 8

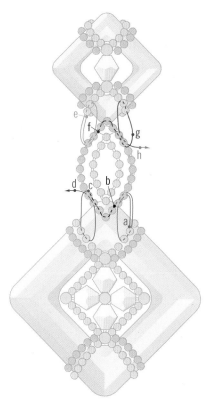

Fig. 9

same corner **(fig. 6)**. Retrace the thread path through the first two loops. Repeat using Bs to add a second set of loops to sit under the loops of As on this corner.

3 Sew through the 4mm and the next 11º on the opposite end of the small crystal square. Repeat step 2 to add two more sets of loops.

4 On the back of the component, sew through the first four As of one of the loops on this end of the small crystal square. Using the tail, sew through the beadwork to exit the corresponding As on the opposite end of the small crystal square, so the working thread exits a loop of As on one end of the square and the tail exits a loop of As on the other end. Don't end the working thread or tail; use these threads to connect bails or links to the components later.

BAILS OR LINKS

1 On 1 yd. (.9 m) of Fireline, pick up 24 Bs, leaving a 6-in. (15cm) tail. Sew through the first 12 Bs, skip the next B in the ring, and sew through the following 11 Bs. Skip the next B, and sew through the following 10 Bs **(fig. 7)**.

2 Pick up an A, skip three Bs in the outer round, and sew through the next nine Bs **(fig. 8, a–b)**. Pick up an A, skip three beads in the outer round, sew through the following nine Bs, and continue through the first A picked up at the start of this step **(b–c)**.

3 Pick up six As, and sew through the A at the opposite end **(c–d)**. Repeat **(d–e)**. Retrace the thread path, skipping the two end As **(e–f)**. End the working thread and tail.

ASSEMBLY

Attach a bail: Position one end of a bail at the top of a large or small component on the back surface. Align two As from one loop on this end to two Bs along one edge of the bail. Using a thread from the component, sew through the corresponding beads **(fig. 9, a–b)**. Sew through the next five Bs, exiting the corresponding Bs on the bail's other edge **(b–c)**. Sew through the corresponding beads **(c–d)**. Retrace the thread path of the join, and end the thread.

Connect two components: Work as for attaching a bail on one end of the link, and then align the remaining link end to the loops on one end of the next component. Use a thread from the next component to sew through the corresponding Bs on this edge of the link **(e–f)**. Sew through the next five Bs to exit the corresponding beads on the other edge of the link **(f–g)**. Sew through the corresponding beads **(g–h)**. Retrace the thread path of the join, and end the thread.

DESIGN IDEAS

Bracelet: Connect small and large components in an alternating pattern for the desired length, with a bail at both ends. Use jump rings to attach a clasp to the end bails.

Earrings: Attach a bail at the top of a large or small component, or connect a few components with links, ending with a bail at the top. Attach earring findings with jump rings.

Pendant: Connect a large and a small component with a link, ending with a bail at the top. Attach to a chain or necklace cord with a jump ring. Attach a bail to both the front and back surfaces of a large or small component to create additional design details. Stitch the top Bs together to create a closed shape. Connect two components with a link on both the front and back surfaces to make the join more secure. This makes the connection stiffer than if only connecting the links to the back, and works best with earrings or pendants.

CROCHET TWO WAYS

Small crochet-tube earrings are a great way to play with an assortment of beads.

MATERIALS

both projects:

- Gudebrod silk thread, size E
- crochet hook, size 8 (1.4mm)
- thin tapestry needle
- chainnose pliers
- roundnose pliers
- wire cutters

fringe earrings

- **14** 4mm bicone crystals
- **2** 4mm silver beads
- **4 g** 2mm silver-plated beads
- **2** 4mm daisy spacers
- **4 g** each:
    cylinder beads
    8º seed beads
    11º seed beads
- pair of earring findings
- **2** bead caps
- **2** 2-in. (5cm) head pins
- beading needles, #12

hoop earrings

- **4** 4mm bicone crystals
- **3 g** 2mm silver-plated beads
- **3 g** each:
    cylinder beads
    8º seed beads
    11º seed beads
- 10 in. (25cm) 20-gauge wire, half-hard
- **4** bead caps

FRINGED EARRINGS

Tube

1 On silk thread, string the following pattern 15 times: two cylinder beads, two 11º seed beads, two 2mm silver beads, and an 8º seed bead. Slide the beads down on the silk so that you have about 24 in. (61cm) of working thread.

2 Leaving an 8-in. (20cm) tail, make a slip stitch. Then make seven bead chain stitches **(photo a)**.

3 Connect the last bead chain stitch to the first by inserting the crochet hook to the left of the first bead **(photo b)**. Push the bead over to the right **(photo c)**, bring the working thread over the previous bead, and slide the next bead down **(photo d)**. Make a bead slip stitch **(photo e)**.

4 Continue working in bead slip stitch until all the beads are used. Work the last row in slip stitch. Cut

the thread about 8 in. from the work and pull the working thread through the loop on your hook.

5 Thread a needle on the tail and secure it using half-hitch knots between the 8ºs. Pull the tail into the next 8º and trim it next to the bead. Repeat with the working thread.

Fringe

1 Secure 1 yd. (.9m) of thread in the beadwork and exit any bead in the end round. Pick up five cylinders, an 8º, a 2mm silver bead, a 4mm bicone crystal, a 2mm silver bead, an 8º, and three cylinders. Skip the cylinders and sew back through the beads to the crocheted tube **(fig., a–b)**.

2 Sew back through the bead the thread was exiting and through the next bead in the end round **(b–c)**.

3 Continue making fringe, adding two extra cylinders each time,

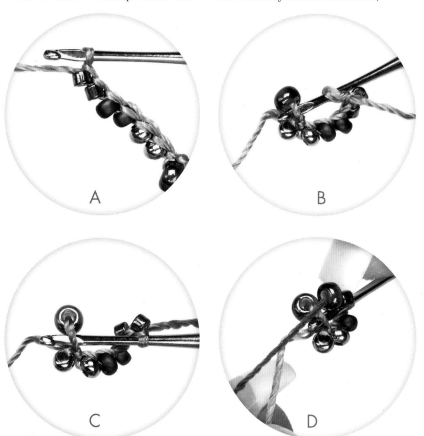

A

B

C

D

until you have a total of seven fringes. End the working thread and tail.

Assembly

1 On a head pin, string a daisy spacer, the crocheted tube (fringe-side first), a bead cap, and a 4mm silver bead **(photo f)**.

2 Make a plain loop above the last bead. Open the loop and attach the earring finding. Close the loop.

3 Make a second earring.

HOOP EARRINGS

1 On silk thread, string the following pattern 37 times: two cylinders, an 11º seed bead, a 2mm silver bead, and an 8º.

2 Leaving an 8-in. tail, make a slip stitch and five bead chain stitches.

3 Repeat step 3 of the tube earring until all the beads are used. End the working thread and tail.

4 Make a plain loop on one end of the wire. String a silver bead, a 4mm bicone crystal, a bead cap, the crocheted tube, a bead cap, a crystal, and a silver bead **(photo g)**. Trim the wire ⅜ in. (1cm) longer than the tube and make a plain loop. Set the remaining wire aside.

5 Bend the tube into a hoop with about ½ in. (1.3cm) between the loops.

6 Cut about 1 in. (2.5cm) off the remaining wire, leaving the rest for the second earring. On the 1-in. piece, make a loop at one end and a 45-degree bend at the other. Curve the wire slightly **(photo h)**. Open the loop and connect it to the hoop **(photo i)**. Close the loop.

7 Make a second earring.

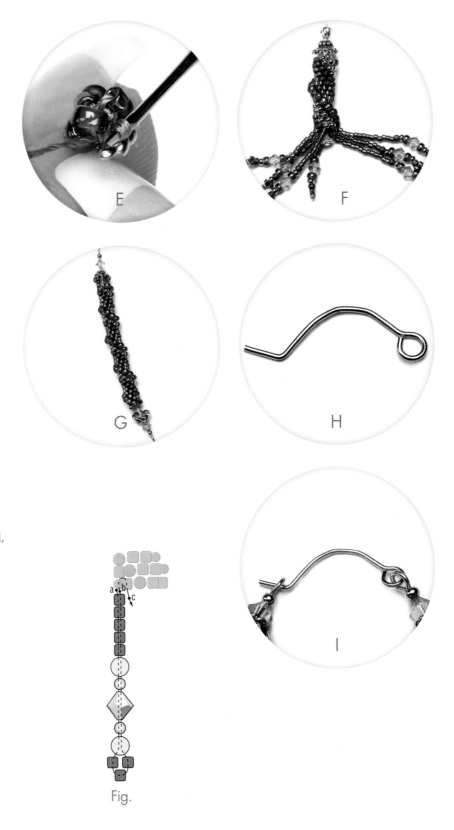

E

F

G

H

a b
c

Fig.

I

EARN YOUR STRIPES

Create a set of striped beaded beads in three graduated sizes; covering wooden beads lets you focus on design and not structure.

Small beaded bead

Large beaded bead

Medium beaded bead

● **TUBULAR PEYOTE STITCH, NETTING**

MATERIALS

one beaded bead

- wooden bead (16mm, 12mm, or 10mm)
- 1 g 11º cylinder beads
- 1 g 15º seed beads in each of **3** colors: A, B, C
- double-sided tape (optional)
- Fireline 6 lb. test
- beading needles, #12

LARGE BEADED BEAD

1 On 2 yd. (1.8 m) of thread, center 40 11º cylinder beads, and tie them into a ring with a square knot. These beads will shift to form the first two rounds as you work the next round. Test that the ring of beads fits around the equator of a 16mm wooden bead. It should be slightly snug to slightly loose.

2 With one end of the thread, stitch a round of tubular peyote stitch using cylinders, and step up through the first bead added in this round. Slip the beadwork around the equator of the wooden bead. If

Fig. 1

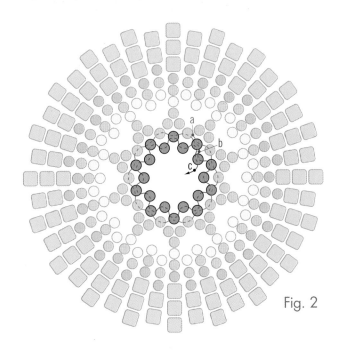

Fig. 2

desired, first wrap the equator with
a strip of double-sided tape to keep
the beadwork in place.

3 On each side of the equator, work
as follows. Alternate sides as you go
to keep your tension even:

> One round of 11º cylinders.
> Two rounds of color A 15º
> seed beads.
> Two rounds of color B 15º
> seed beads.
> Two rounds of color C 15º
> seed beads.

As you work the rounds of 15ºs,
take advantage of the size variations
between the beads and select the
largest As, average-sized Bs, and
smallest Cs.

4 On each side of the bead, work a
round of modified netting to
decrease the number of stitches in
the round: Pick up five Bs, skip the
next three Cs, sew through the
following C in the round, and sew
back through the last B just picked
up **(fig. 1, a–b)**.

5 Pick up four Bs, skip the next
three Cs, sew through the following
C, and sew back through the last B
picked up **(b–c)**. Repeat this stitch
until there is one stitch remaining in
the round **(c–d)**.

6 To complete the round, pick up
three Bs, and sew down through
the first B picked up in the first stitch
of this round. Sew through the
corresponding C in the previous
round, and sew back through the
first three Bs added in the first stitch
of this round **(d–e)**.

7 Pick up an A, and sew through
the middle B in the next stitch.
Repeat to complete the round, and
step up through the first A added in
this round **(fig. 2, a–b)**.

8 For the final round, pick up an
A, and sew through the next A in
the previous round. Repeat to
complete the round **(b–c)**, and
end the threads.

MEDIUM BEADED BEAD

Work as in "Large Beaded Bead"
with the following changes:

In step 1, begin with 1½ yd. (1.4 m)
of thread, and use 36 11º cylinders
and a 12mm wooden bead.

In step 3, omit the first round of
cylinders on each side, and then
work two rounds with A 15ºs and
two rounds with B 15ºs. Do not
work two rounds with C 15ºs.

In steps 4–6, work the round of
modified netting with C 15ºs.

Work step 7 using As.

In the final round, pick up an A,
and sew through the next two As
in the previous round. Repeat three
times, and then work one more
regular peyote stitch. Note: Because
the number of beads in the original
ring was not evenly divisible by four,
the decrease doesn't work out
perfectly. However, since the
decrease is at the end of the bead,
it is not noticeable without close
inspection. Retrace the thread path
through the final round to draw the
work in tight around the opening of
the bead. End the threads.

SMALL BEADED BEAD

Work as in "Large Beaded Bead"
with the following changes:

In step 1, begin with 1 yd. (.9 m) of
thread, and use 28 11º cylinders and
a 10mm wooden bead.

In step 3, skip the first round of
cylinders on each side, and then
work one round with A 15ºs and two
rounds with B 15ºs. Do not work
two rounds with C 15ºs.

In steps 4–6, work the round of
modified netting with C 15ºs.

Work as in step 7 for the final
round. Retrace the thread path
through the last round, and end
the threads.

A

B

C

D

CROCHETED ROPE

1 Thread a twisted wire needle on the upholstery thread. To make the green necklace, string a 6mm pearl, a 4mm pearl, a 5mm bicone, a 4mm pearl, and a 4mm bicone. Omit the second 4mm pearl if you are making the burgundy necklace. Repeat the bead sequence until you have used all the beads. Do not cut the thread off the spool until you are finished with the crochet.

2 Leaving an 8-in (20cm) tail, work five chain stitches to start the green necklace and four to start the burgundy necklace. Connect the last chain to the first with a slipstitch **(fig. 1)**.

3 Work a round of bead slip-stitches **(fig. 2)** into the round of chain stitches.

4 For the next round, insert the hook to the left of the first bead

and push the bead over to the right **(photo a)**. Bring the thread over the bead in the first round **(photo b)**. Slide down a bead and work a slip-stitch **(photo c)**.

5 Repeat to complete the round. Continue to add rounds, working counterclockwise, using all the beads strung. The beads will automatically form a spiral.

6 Work a round of slipstitches to complete the rope, then pull the thread through until you have an 18-in. (46cm) tail. Cut the thread.

7 Thread a tapestry needle on the 8-in. tail. Weave the tail into the crocheted rope, tying half-hitch knots between a few beads. Trim the tail.

8 Green necklace: Thread a tapestry needle on the 18-in. tail. To make the loop, pick up 12 4mm pearls and sew into the last round of slipstitches **(photo d)**. Reinforce

● **BEAD CROCHET, FRINGE**

MATERIALS

both necklaces

- upholstery thread to match beads
- twisted wire needles
- crochet hook, size 7
- tapestry needle
- beading needles, #10 and #12
- Fireline 6 lb. test

green crochet rope

- **64** each of the following: 6mm faceted pearls, 5mm bicone crystals, 4mm bicone crystals
- **130** 4mm crystal pearls

fringe

- **100** (approx.) each of the following: 6mm faceted pearls, 5mm crystal bicones, 4mm crystal bicones
- **200** (approx.) 4mm crystal pearls
- hank or tube of any style of seed bead 10º–12º
- **3** small art-glass beads
- **5** 6mm crystal rondelles
- **6** top-drilled crystal drops

burgundy crochet rope

- **109** each of the following: 6mm faceted pearls, 5mm crystal bicones, 4mm crystal bicones
- **124** 4mm crystal pearls
- medium to large art-glass bead

fringe

- **100** (approx.) each of the following: 6mm faceted pearls, 5mm bicone crystals, 4mm bicone crystals, 4mm crystal pearls, 3mm crystal pearls
- hank or tube of any style of seed bead, 10º–12º
- **14** 8mm round crystals

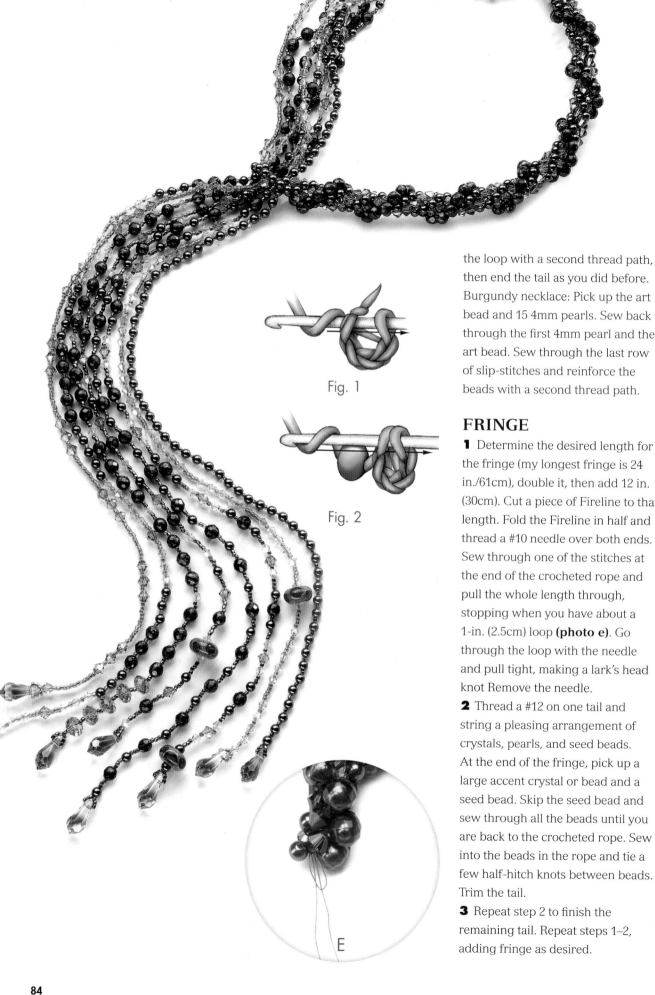

Fig. 1

Fig. 2

the loop with a second thread path, then end the tail as you did before. Burgundy necklace: Pick up the art bead and 15 4mm pearls. Sew back through the first 4mm pearl and the art bead. Sew through the last row of slip-stitches and reinforce the beads with a second thread path.

FRINGE

1 Determine the desired length for the fringe (my longest fringe is 24 in./61cm), double it, then add 12 in. (30cm). Cut a piece of Fireline to that length. Fold the Fireline in half and thread a #10 needle over both ends. Sew through one of the stitches at the end of the crocheted rope and pull the whole length through, stopping when you have about a 1-in. (2.5cm) loop **(photo e)**. Go through the loop with the needle and pull tight, making a lark's head knot Remove the needle.

2 Thread a #12 on one tail and string a pleasing arrangement of crystals, pearls, and seed beads. At the end of the fringe, pick up a large accent crystal or bead and a seed bead. Skip the seed bead and sew through all the beads until you are back to the crocheted rope. Sew into the beads in the rope and tie a few half-hitch knots between beads. Trim the tail.

3 Repeat step 2 to finish the remaining tail. Repeat steps 1–2, adding fringe as desired.

E

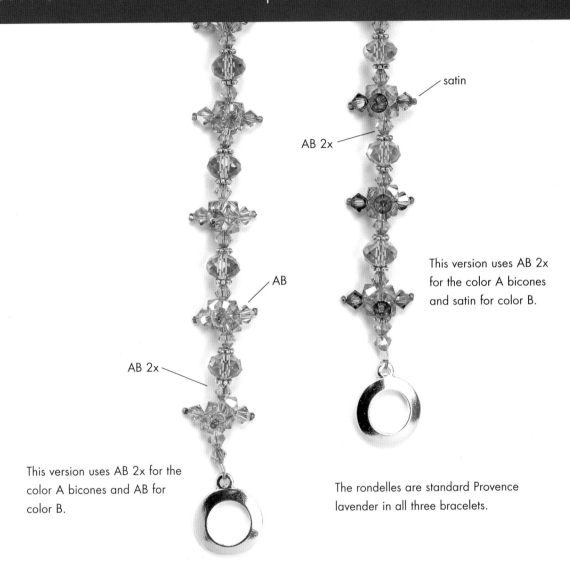

satin

AB 2x

AB

AB 2x

This version uses AB 2x for the color A bicones and satin for color B.

This version uses AB 2x for the color A bicones and AB for color B.

The rondelles are standard Provence lavender in all three bracelets.

● PICOT TECHNIQUE, STRINGING

MATERIALS

bracelet
- **7–8** 8mm rondelle crystals in color A, B, or C
- **74–84** 4mm bicone crystals, color A
- **24–27** 4mm bicone crystals, color B
- **21–24** 15º seed beads
- **14–16** flat spacers
- flexible beading wire, .010 or .012
- **2** crimp beads
- toggle clasp
- chainnose or crimping pliers
- diagonal wire cutters

earrings
- **2** 8mm rondelle crystals
- **8** 4mm bicone crystals
- 4-loop spacer bar
- **6** 1½-in. (3.8cm) head pins
- pair of earring wires
- chainnose and roundnose pliers
- diagonal wire cutters

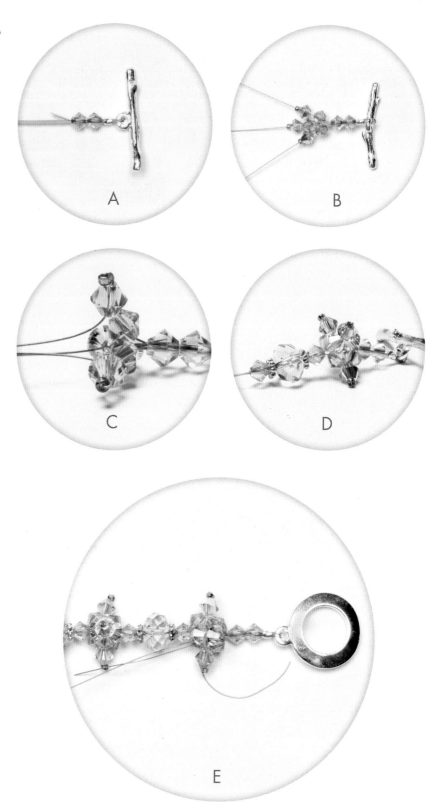

BRACELET

1 Cut three 24-in. (61cm) pieces of beading wire. Over all three wires, string two color A bicone crystals, a crimp bead, and half of a toggle clasp. Go back through the beads just strung and tighten the wire. Crimp the crimp bead and trim the excess wire **(photo a)**.

2 On each wire, string a color A bicone, a color B bicone, and a 15º seed bead **(photo b)**.

3 With each wire, go back through the color B **(photo c)**.

4 a On each wire, string a color A.
b Over all three wires, string: color A, flat spacer, rondelle, flat spacer, color A **(photo d)**.

F

G

H

I

Q: How do crystal finishes differ?
– *Dianne*

A: AB (aurora borealis) is an iridescent coating that adds a multicolored effect. The AB finish is normally applied to half of a bead. AB 2x means the coating has been applied to the entire bead.

The AB version of Provence lavender is very similar to the standard crystal. The AB 2x is a more pronounced iridescence.

The satin finish gives the crystal a darker appearance.

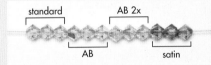

c Repeat steps 2 to 4b until the strands are within 2 in. (5cm) of the finished length.

5 Repeat steps 2 to 4a. Over all wires, string: a color A, a crimp bead, and a clasp half. Go back through the beads just strung and tighten the wires. Crimp the crimp bead. Trim the wire **(photo e)**.

EARRINGS

1 On a head pin, string a bicone crystal, a rondelle, and a bicone. Make a plain loop. On a head pin, string a bicone. Make a plain loop. Make two bicone units **(photo f)**.

2 Use wire cutters to cut a four-loop spacer bar in half **(photo g)**.

3 Open the loop of the rondelle unit and attach a loop of a spacer-bar half. Close the loop. Attach a bicone unit to each spacer-bar loop **(photo h)**.

4 Open an earring wire loop and attach the dangle. Close the loop **(photo i)**.

STITCHED CRYSTAL EARRINGS

This rhythmic stitching pattern provides contrast as well as balance.

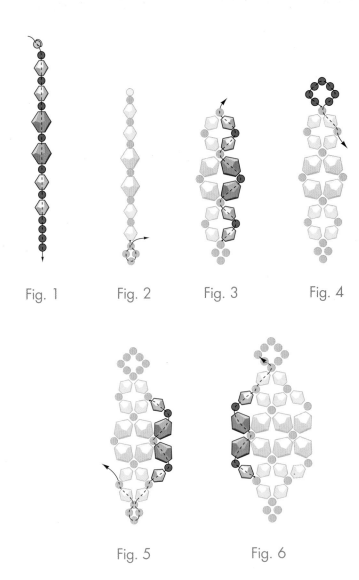

Fig. 1   Fig. 2   Fig. 3   Fig. 4

Fig. 5   Fig. 6

● NETTING, STRINGING
MATERIALS
blue earrings
- **16** 4mm bicone crystals
- **24** 3mm bicone crystals
- 1 g 11º seed beads
- Fireline, 6 lb. test
- beading needle, #12
- pair of earring wires
- chainnose and roundnose pliers

gold earrings
- **44** 3mm bicone crystals
- 1 g cylinder beads
- flexible beading wire, .014–.015
- **2** crimp beads
- pair of earring wires
- chainnose pliers
- crimping pliers

BLUE EARRINGS

1 For each earring: Cut a 1-yd. (.9 m) piece of Fireline. String a stopper bead, leaving a 6-in. (15 cm) tail. Pick up: 11º seed bead, 3mm bicone crystal, 11º, 3mm, 11º, 4mm bicone crystal, 11º, 4mm, 11º, 3mm, 11º, 3mm, four 11ºs **(fig. 1)**.

2 Skipping the last three 11ºs, sew back through the next 11º to create a picot at the end of the row **(fig. 2)**.

3 Pick up a 3mm, an 11º, and a 3mm. Skip the 3mm, 11º, and 3mm in the previous row, and sew through the next 11º. Pick up a 4mm, an 11º, and a 4mm. Skip the 4mm, 11º, and 4mm in the previous row, and sew through the next 11º. Pick up a 3mm, an 11º, and a 3mm. Skip the 3mm, 11º and 3mm in the previous row, and sew through the next 11º **(fig. 3)**.

4 Pick up seven 11ºs, and sew back through the 11º your thread exited at the end of step 3. Sew through the 3mm and the next 11º as shown **(fig. 4)**.

5 a Pick up a 3mm, an 11º, and a 4mm. Skip the 3mm, 11º, and 4mm in the previous row, and sew through the next 11º.

b Pick up a 4mm, an 11º, and a 3mm. Skip the 4mm, 11º, and 3mm, and sew through the next 11º, 3mm, four 11ºs, 3mm, and 11º **(fig. 5)**.

6 Repeat step 5a on the other side. Pick up a 4mm, an 11º, and a 3mm. Skip the 4mm, 11º, and 3mm, and sew through the next 11º, 3mm, and 11º **(fig. 6)**.

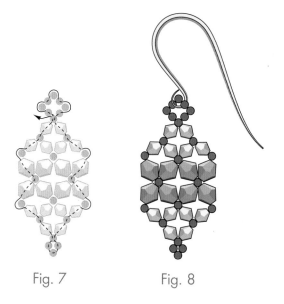

Fig. 7   Fig. 8

7 Retrace the outer edge of the earring by sewing through all the beads on the perimeter, skipping every other 11º in the loop and the four outer 11ºs **(fig. 7)**.

8 Remove the stopper bead and tie a square knot. Open the loop of an earring wire and attach the dangle. Close the loop **(fig. 8)**. Make a second earring

GOLD EARRINGS

1 Cut a 2-ft. (61cm) length of beading wire. Center three cylinder beads on the wire. Hold the ends together and string a crystal and a cylinder over both strands **(photo a)**.

2 On one end, string a crystal, a cylinder, a crystal, and seven cylinders. Go back through the first cylinder strung in this step and pull the beads into a tight ring. Repeat with the other strand **(photo b)**.

3 String a crystal on each strand and a cylinder over both strands **(photo c)**.

4 On one strand, string a crystal, a cylinder, a crystal, and seven cylinders. Go back through the second cylinder added in step 2. String a crystal and go through the first cylinder added in this step. Repeat with the other strand **(photo d)**.

A

B

C

D

E

F

Q: How do you come up with new ideas for your designs?
—Jennifer

A: Creativity takes time! When I can, I experiment away from my tried-and-true favorites. Here are some ideas for you:

• Try a stitch in some beads you normally wouldn't choose. I love the way triangle beads nestle together, changing the basic stitch because the beads won't behave like round ones. Grouping beads on your work surface can help you fit the beads together like a puzzle, and also choose your colors better than if they were left in tubes or bags.
• Master the techniques. Adding and ending the threads, crimping like a pro, and working even stitches make all the difference when designing. Give attention to the details. Take the time to really think your jewelry design through.
• Take a class. When I get a chance to take a class, I am amazed by how inspiring it is. Observing master instructors teach, the way they utilize their tools, or the expertise they exhibit with their color palette make it really worthwhile. Also listen to fellow students. Many of them may have been working with beads long enough that their own beading wisdom enhances the class.
• Go easy on yourself. If something doesn't work out, try again. It takes time to get it right.

5 Repeat step 3 **(photo e)**.
6 On one strand, string a crystal and seven cylinders. Go through the second cylinder added in step 4. String a crystal and go through the first cylinder added in this step. Repeat with the other strand.
7 Repeat step 3, then string a crystal and a crimp bead. Go back through the crimp bead, tighten the wire to create a small loop **(photo f)**, and crimp the crimp bead.
8 Open the loop on an earring wire and attach the earring. Make a second earring.

SPECTACULAR RING

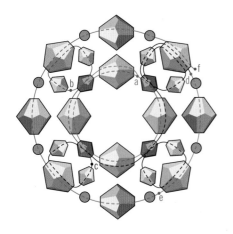

Fig. 1

Fig. 2

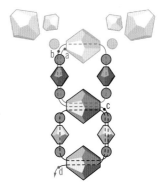

Fig. 3

RING TOP

1 On 2 yd. (1.8m) of Fireline, alternate four 4mm color A bicone crystals and four 3mm color C bicone crystals leaving a 10-in. (25cm) tail. Tie them into a ring with a square knot. Sew through the next A and C **(fig. 1, a–b)**.

2 Pick up a 3mm color D bicone crystal, an A, and a D. Sew back through the C your thread exited at the start of this step, and then continue on through the next A and C in the ring **(b–c)**.

3 Repeat step 2 three times, then continue through the next D and A **(c–d)**.

4 Pick up a 15º seed bead, a 4mm color B bicone crystal, and a 15º. Sew through the next A **(d–e)**.

5 Repeat step 4 three times **(e–f)**, and then reinforce the new bottom ring, exiting a B. Set the working thread aside, and pick up the tail, making sure the tail is exiting an A.

6 Pick up a 15º, a D, a C, a D, and a 15º. Sew back through the A that your thread exited at the start of this step, and continue around the ring, exiting the opposite A **(fig. 2, a–b)**.

7 Pick up a 15º and a D. Sew through the C from step 6 **(b–c)**. Pick up a D and a 15º, and sew back through the A. Continue on through the next C and A **(c–d)**. Secure the tail using half-hitch knots between a few beads. Trim the tail.

RING BAND

1 With the working thread, pick up a 15º, a C, a 15º, an A, a 15º, a C, and a 15º. Sew through the B from the ring top **(fig. 3, a–b)**. Then sew through the 15º, the C, the 15º, and the A **(b–c)**.

2 Repeat step 1, using Ds instead of Cs and a B instead of an A **(c–d)**.

3 Repeat steps 1 and 2 nine times or until you reach the desired size.

4 To connect the band's last row, pick up a 15º, a C, and a 15º. Sew through the opposite B on the ring top. Pick up a 15º, a C, and a 15º. Sew through the D on the ring band.

5 Reinforce the band with another thread path, and secure the working thread.

● **MODIFIED RIGHT-ANGLE WEAVE**
MATERIALS
one ring
- 4mm bicone crystals
    - 13 color A
    - 8 color B
- 3mm bicone crystals
    - 17 color C
    - 20 color D
- 1 g 15º seed beads
- Fireline 6 lb. test
- beading needles, #12

Note: For a larger ring top, substitute 6mm crystals for colors A and B and 4mm crystals for colors C and D in steps 1–5. Keep the crystals the same in steps 6 and 7.

A

B

C

D

● STRINGING

MATERIALS

- both projects
- flexible beading wire, .012–.015
- **2** pairs of pliers
- crimping pliers
- wire cutters

necklace 17–26 in. (43–66cm)

- **250–300** 12mm bugle beads
- **60–100** 6mm bicone crystals
- **5 g** 11º seed beads
- **3 g** 15º seed beads
- clasp
- **2** 8mm jump rings
- **10** crimp beads
- **10** crimp covers (optional)

bracelet 8 in. (20cm)

- **80–100** 12mm bugle beads
- bicone crystals:
     8 6mm
     16 4mm
- **2 g** 11º seed beads
- **1 g** 15º seed beads
- clasp
- **2** 8mm jump rings
- **8–12** crimp beads
- **8–12** crimp covers (optional)

NECKLACE

1 Cut a piece of beading wire twice as long as the desired length of your first strand.

2 On one end, string a crimp bead and 13 15º seed beads. Go back through the crimp bead, making a small loop. Crimp the crimp bead **(photo a)**, and trim the short tail.

3 String an 11º seed bead, a 12mm bugle bead, two 11ºs, and a 15º. Skip the 15º, and go back through the last 11º **(photo b)**.

4 To add a crystal accent, pick up an 11º, a 6mm bicone crystal, an 11º, a 6mm, two 11ºs, and a 15º. Skip the 15º, and go back through the last 11º **(photo c)**.

5 Work as in steps 3 and 4 until you achieve the desired length. In my necklace, I made a random pattern of several bugles and then a crystal accent.

6 String a crimp bead and 13 15ºs. Go back through the crimp bead, and crimp it. Close a crimp cover over each crimp if desired.

7 Repeat steps 1–6 for a total of five strands, varying the length of the strands and the pattern of bugles and crystals.

8 Open a jump ring, and attach the clasp and a loop on one end of each strand **(photo d)**. Close the jump ring. Repeat on the other end.

BRACELET

Follow the instructions for "Necklace" with the following changes: In step 4, pick up an 11º, a 4mm bicone crystal, an 8mm bicone crystal, a 4mm, two 11ºs, and a 15º; in step 7, make a total of four to six strands.

TIP

If you'd prefer to use a multistrand clasp, omit the loops of 15ºs at the ends of the strands, and crimp the wire loops to the clasp.

TIPS

• Use shorter bugles for a dainty version of this necklace or bracelet.
• Make only one strand, or try out different numbers of strands until you're pleased with the results.
• Vary the number of crystals, depending on how casual or dressy you would like your jewelry to be.

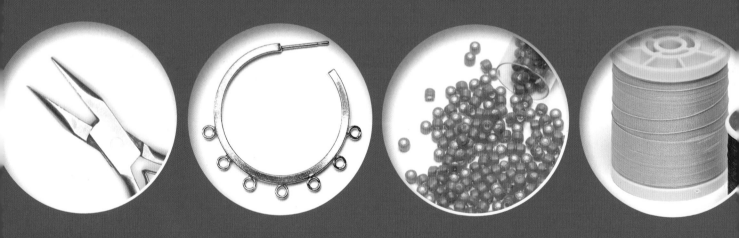

BASICS

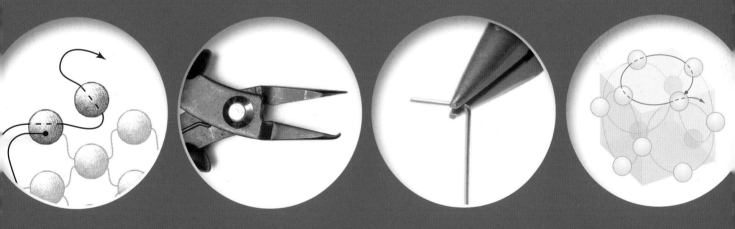

chainnose pliers

roundnose pliers

wire cutters

crimping pliers

split-ring pliers

Tools & Materials

Excellent tools and materials for making jewelry are available in bead and craft stores, through catalogs, and online. Here are the essential supplies you'll need for the projects in this book.

Tools

Chainnose pliers have smooth, flat inner jaws, and the tips taper to a point. Use them for gripping, bending wire, and for opening and closing loops and jump rings.

Roundnose pliers have smooth, tapered, conical jaws used to make loops. The closer to the tip you work, the smaller the loop will be.

Use the front of a **wire cutters'** blades to make a pointed cut and the back of the blades to make a flat cut.

Crimping pliers have two grooves in their jaws that are used to fold and roll a crimp bead into a compact shape.

Make it easier to open split rings by inserting the curved jaw of **split-ring pliers** between the wires.

Beading needles are coded by size. The higher the number, the finer the beading needle. Unlike sewing needles, the eye of a beading needle is almost as narrow as its shaft. In addition to the size of the bead, the number of times you will pass through the bead also affects the needle size that you will use; if you will pass through a bead multiple times, you need to use a thinner needle.

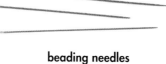

beading needles

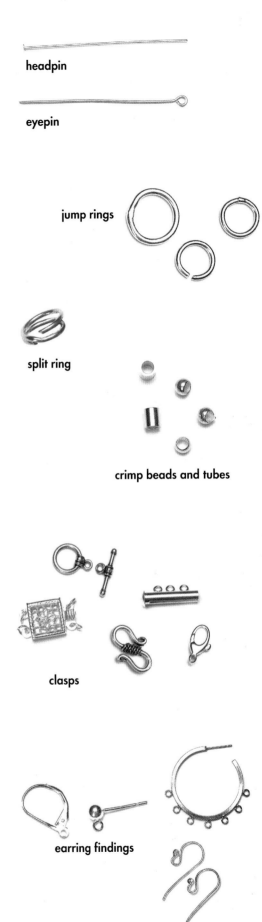

headpin

eyepin

jump rings

split ring

crimp beads and tubes

clasps

earring findings

Findings

A **headpin** looks like a long, blunt, thick sewing pin. It has a flat or decorative head on one end to keep beads on. Headpins come in different diameters (gauges) and lengths.

Eyepins are like headpins except they have a round loop on one end instead of a head. Make your own eye pins from wire.

A **jump ring** is used to connect components. It is a small wire circle or oval that is either soldered closed or comes with a cut so it can be opened and closed.

Split rings are used like jump rings but are much more secure. They look like tiny key rings and are made of springy wire.

Crimp beads and tubes are small, large-holed, thin-walled metal beads designed to be flattened or crimped into a tight roll. Use them when stringing jewelry on flexible beading wire.

Clasps come in many sizes and shapes. Some of the most common (clockwise from the top left) are the toggle, consisting of a ring and a bar; slide, consisting of one tube that slides inside another; lobster claw, which opens when you pull on a tiny lever; S-hook, which links two soldered jump rings or split rings; and box, with a tab and a slot.

Earring findings come in a huge variety of metals and styles, including (from left to right) lever back, post, hoop, and French hook. You will almost always want a loop (or loops) on earring findings so you can attach beads.

Stitching and Stringing Materials

Selecting beading thread and cord is one of the most important decisions you'll make when planning a project. Review the descriptions below to evaluate which material is best for your design.

Threads come in many sizes and strengths. Size (diameter or thickness) is designated by a letter or number. OO and A/O are the thinnest; B, D, E, F, and FF are subsequently thicker. **Cord** is measured on a number scale; 0 corresponds in thickness to D-size thread, 1 equals E, 2 equals F, and 3 equals FF.

Parallel filament nylon, such as Nymo or C-Lon, is made from many thin nylon fibers that are extruded and heat-set to form a single-ply thread. Parallel filament nylon is durable and easy to thread, but it can be prone to fraying and stretching. It is best used in beadweaving and bead embroidery.

Plied nylon thread, such as Silamide, is made from two or more nylon threads that are extruded, twisted together, and coated or bonded for further strength, making them strong and durable. It is more resistant to fraying than parallel filament nylon, and some brands do not stretch. It's a good material for twisted fringe, bead crochet, and beadwork that needs a lot of body.

Plied gel-spun polyethylene (GSP), such as Power Pro or DandyLine, is made from polyethylene fibers that have been spun into two or more threads that are braided together. It is almost unbreakable, it doesn't stretch, and

flexible beading wire

nylon threads

it resists fraying. The thickness can make it difficult to make multiple passes through a bead. It is ideal for stitching with larger beads, such as pressed glass and crystals.

Parallel filament GSP, such as Fireline, is a single-ply thread made from spun and bonded polyethylene fibers. It's extremely strong, it doesn't stretch, and it resists fraying. However, crystals will cut through parallel filament GSP, and smoke-colored varieties can leave a black residue on hands and beads. It's most appropriate for bead stitching.

Polyester thread, such as Gutermann, is made from polyester fibers that are spun into single yarns and then twisted into plied thread. It doesn't stretch and comes in many colors, but it can become fuzzy with use. It is best for bead crochet or bead embroidery when the thread must match the fabric.

Flexible beading wire is composed of wires twisted together and covered with nylon. This wire is stronger than thread and does not stretch. The higher the number of inner strands (between 3 and 49), the more flexible and kink-resistant the wire. It is available in a variety of sizes. Use .014 and .015 for stringing most gemstones, crystals, and glass beads. Use thicker varieties, .018, .019, and .024, for heavy beads or nuggets. Use thinner wire, .010 and .012, for lightweight pieces and beads with very small holes, such as pearls. The thinnest wires can also be used for some bead-stitching projects.

parallel filament GSP

Seed Beads

A huge variety of beads is available, but the beads most commonly used in the projects in this book are seed beads. Seed beads come in packages, tubes, and hanks. A standard hank (a looped bundle of beads strung on thread) contains 12 20-in. (51 cm) strands, but vintage hanks are often much smaller. Tubes and packages are usually measured in grams and vary in size. Seed beads have been manufactured in many sizes ranging from the largest, 2°, 5°, (also called "E beads"), which are about 5 mm wide, to tiny size 20° or 22°, which aren't much larger than grains of sand. (The symbol $^{\circ}$ stands for "aught" or "zero." The greater the number of aughts, e.g., 22°, the smaller the bead.) Beads smaller than Japanese 15°s have not been produced for the past 100 years, but vintage beads can be found in limited sizes and colors. The most commonly available size in the widest range of colors is 11°.

Most round seed beads are made in Japan and the Czech Republic. Czech seed beads are slightly irregular and rounder than Japanese seed beads, which are uniform in size and a bit squared off. Czech beads give a bumpier surface when woven, but they reflect light at a wider range of angles. Japanese seed beads produce a uniform surface and texture. Japanese and Czech seed beads can be used together, but a Japanese seed bead is slightly larger than the same size Czech seed bead. Seed beads also come in sparkly cut versions. Japanese hex-cut or hex beads are formed with six sides. 2- or 3-cut Czech beads are less regular. Charlottes have an irregular facet cut on one side of the bead. Japanese cylinder beads, otherwise known as Delicas (the Miyuki brand name), Toho Treasures (the brand name of Toho), and Toho Aikos are extremely popular for peyote stitch projects. These beads are very regular and have large holes, which are useful for stitches requiring multiple thread passes. The beads fit together almost seamlessly,

producing a smooth, fabric-like surface. Bugle beads are thin glass tubes. They can be sized by number or length, depending on where they are made. Japanese size 1 bugles are about 2 mm long, but bugles can be made even longer than 30 mm. They can be hex-cut, straight, or twisted, but the selection of colors, sizes, shapes, and finishes is limited. Seed beads also come in a variety of other shapes, including triangles, cubes, and drops.

In stitches where the beads meet each other end to end or side by side — peyote stitch, brick stitch, and square stitch — try using Japanese cylinder beads to achieve a smooth, flat surface. For a more textured surface, use Czech or round Japanese seed beads. For right-angle weave, in which groups of four or more beads form circular stitches, the rounder the seed bead, the better; otherwise you risk having gaps. Round seed beads also are better for netting and strung jewelry.

seed beads

cube beads

triangle beads

drop beads

hex-cut beads

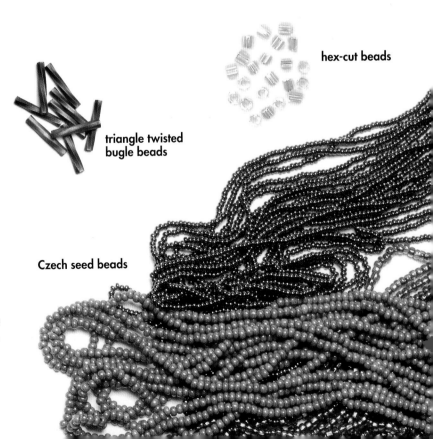

triangle twisted bugle beads

Czech seed beads

Techniques

CRIMPING

Use crimping pliers and crimp beads to secure the ends of flexible beading wire:

1 Position the crimp bead in the notch closest to the handle of the crimping pliers. Hold the wires apart to make sure one wire is on each side of the dent, and squeeze the pliers to compress the crimp bead.

2 Position the crimp bead in the notch near the tip of the pliers with the dent facing the tips. Squeeze the pliers to fold the crimp in half. Tug on the wires to make sure the crimp is secure.

OPENING AND CLOSING PLAIN LOOPS, JUMP RINGS, AND EARRING FINDINGS

1 Hold a loop or a jump ring with two pairs of pliers.

2 To open the loop or jump ring, bring the tips of one pair of pliers toward you, and push the tips of the other pair away from you. Reverse the steps to close.

 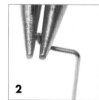

MAKING A PLAIN LOOP

1 Using chainnose pliers, make a right-angle bend approximately ¼ in. (6mm) from the end of the wire.

2 Grip the tip of the wire with roundnose pliers. Press downward slightly, and rotate the wire into a loop. The closer to the tip of the pliers you work, the smaller the loop will be.

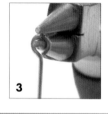

3 Let go, then grip the loop at the same place on the pliers, and keep turning to close the loop.

MAKING A WRAPPED LOOP

1 Using chainnose pliers, make a right-angle bend approximately 1¼ in. (3.2cm) from the end of the wire.

2 Position the jaws of the roundnose pliers in the bend.

3 Curve the short end of the wire over the top jaw of the pliers.

4 Reposition the pliers so the lower jaw fits snugly in the loop. Curve the wire downward around the bottom jaw of the pliers. This is the first half of a wrapped loop.

5 To complete the wraps, grasp the top of the loop with chainnose pliers.

6 Wrap the wire around the stem two or three times. Trim the excess wire, and gently press the cut end close to the wraps with chainnose pliers.

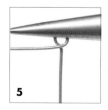 

STOP BEAD

Use a stop bead to secure beads temporarily as you begin stitching. Choose a bead that is distinct from the beads in your project. String the stop bead, and sew through it again in the same direction. For extra security, sew through it again.

ADDING AND ENDING THREAD

To add a thread, sew into the beadwork several rows prior to the point where the last bead was added. Weave through the beadwork, following the existing thread path. Tie a few half-hitch knots between beads, and exit where the last stitch ended. To end a thread, weave back into the beadwork, following the existing thread path and tying two or three half-hitch knots between beads as you go. Change directions as you weave so the thread crosses itself. Sew through a few beads after the last knot, and trim the thread.

HALF-HITCH KNOT

Pass the needle under the thread between two beads. A loop will form as you pull the thread through. Cross back over the thread between the beads, sew through the loop, and pull gently to draw the knot into the beadwork.

SQUARE KNOT

Bring the left-hand thread over the right-hand thread and around. Cross right over left, and go through the loop.

SURGEON'S KNOT

Bring the left-hand thread over the right-hand thread twice. Pull the ends to tighten. Cross right over left, and go through the loop. Tighten.

LARK'S HEAD KNOT

Fold a cord in half and lay it behind a ring, loop, bar, etc. with the fold pointing down. Bring the ends through the ring from back to front, then through the fold and tighten.

OVERHAND KNOT

Cross the ends to make a loop. Bring the end that crosses in front behind the loop, and pull it through the loop to the front. Tighten.

CROSSWEAVE TECHNIQUE

Crossweave is a beading technique in which you string one or more beads on both ends of a length of thread or cord and then cross the ends through one or more beads.

CROCHET

Chain stitch

Make a loop in the thread, crossing the ball end over the tail. Put the hook through the loop, yarn over the hook, and draw through the first loop. Yarn over the hook, and draw through the loop. Repeat for the desired number of chain stitches.

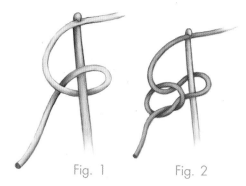

Fig. 1   Fig. 2

Slip stitch

Go into the next stitch. Yarn over, and draw the yarn through the stitch and the loop.

HERRINGBONE STITCH

Flat strip

1 Work the first row in ladder stitch (see "Ladder stitch: Making a ladder") to the desired length, exiting the top of the last bead added.

2 Pick up two beads, and sew down through the next bead in the previous row **(fig. 1, a–b)**. Sew up through the following bead in the previous row, pick up two beads, and sew down through the next bead **(b–c)**. Repeat across the first row.

3 To turn to start the next row, sew down through the end bead in the previous row and back through the last bead of the pair just added **(fig. 2, a–b)**. Pick up two beads, sew down through the next bead in the previous row, and sew up through the following bead **(b–c)**. Continue adding pairs of beads across the row.

4 To turn without having thread show on the edge, pick up an accent or smaller bead before you sew back through the last bead of the pair you just added, or work the "Concealed turn" below.

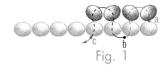

Fig. 1

Fig. 2

Concealed turn

To hide the thread on the edge without adding a bead for each turn, sew up through the second-to-last bead in the previous row, and continue through the last bead added **(a–b)**. Pick up two beads, sew down through the next bead in the previous row, and sew up through the following bead **(b–c)**. Continue adding pairs of beads across the row. Using this turn will flatten the angle of the edge beads, making the edge stacks look a little different than the others.

Fig. 1

Fig. 2

LADDER STITCH

Making a ladder

1 Pick up two beads, and sew through them both again, positioning the beads side by side so that their holes are parallel **(fig. 1, a–b)**.

2 Add subsequent beads by picking up one bead, sewing through the previous bead, then sewing through the new bead **(b–c)**. Continue for the desired length.

This technique produces uneven tension, which you can correct by zigzagging back through the beads in the opposite direction **(fig. 2)**, or by using the "Crossweave method" below.

Crossweave method

1 Thread a needle on each end of a length of thread, and center a bead.

2 Working in crossweave technique (see "Crossweave technique"), pick up a bead with one needle, and cross the other needle through it **(a–b** and **aa–bb)**. Add all subsequent beads in the same manner.

NETTING

Netting produces airy, flexible beadwork that resembles a net and can be worked vertically, horizontally, or in the round (tubular netting). Netting starts with a base row or round of beads upon which subsequent rows or rounds are stitched. Subsequent rows or rounds are added by picking up a given odd number of beads, and sewing through the center bead of the next stitch in the previous row or round.

Instructions for netting vary for each project, but some common variations include three-, five-, and seven-bead netting. The number of beads per stitch determines the drape of the overall piece. More beads per stitch produce larger spaces and a more fluid drape.

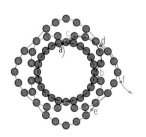

Tubular netting

1 Pick up 24 11ºs, and sew through them again to form a ring, exiting the first 11º picked up.

2 Pick up five 11ºs, skip five 11ºs in the ring, and sew through the next 11º in the ring **(a–b)**. Repeat to complete the round **(b–c)**. Step up through the first three 11ºs in the first stitch **(c–d)**.

3 Pick up five 11ºs, skip five 11ºs in the previous round, and sew through the center 11º in the next stitch in the previous round **(d–e)**. Repeat to complete the round, and step up through three 11ºs in the first stitch **(e–f)**.

4 Repeat step 3 to complete the sample.

PEYOTE STITCH

Flat even-count

1 Pick up an even number of beads **(a–b)**. These beads will shift to form the first two rows.

2 To begin row 3, pick up a bead, skip the last bead picked up in the previous step, and sew back through the next bead **(b–c)**. For each stitch, pick up a bead, skip a bead in the previous row, and sew through the next bead, exiting the first bead picked up **(c–d)**. The beads added in this row are higher than the previous rows and are referred to as "up-beads."

3 For each stitch in subsequent rows, pick up a bead, and sew through the next up-bead in the previous row **(d–e)**. To count peyote stitch rows, count the total number of beads along both straight edges.

Flat odd-count

Odd-count peyote is the same as even-count peyote, except for the turn on odd-numbered rows, where the last bead of the row can't be attached in the usual way because there is no up-bead to sew through.

Work the traditional odd-row turn as follows:

1 Begin as for flat even-count peyote, but pick up an odd number of beads. Work row 3 as in even-count, stopping before adding the last two beads.

2 Work a figure-8 turn at the end of row 3: Pick up the next-to-last bead (#7), and sew through #2, then #1 **(a–b)**. Pick up the last bead of the row (#8), and sew through #2, #3, #7, #2, #1, and #8 **(b–c)**.

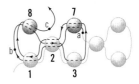

Fig. 1

You can work this turn at the end of each odd-numbered row, but this edge will be stiffer than the other. Instead, in subsequent odd-numbered rows, pick up the last bead of the row, then sew under the thread bridge immediately below. Sew back through the last bead added to begin the next row.

Fig. 2

Circular

Circular peyote is also worked in continuous rounds like tubular peyote, but the rounds stay flat and radiate outward from the center as a result of increases or using larger beads. If the rounds do not increase, the beadwork will become tubular.

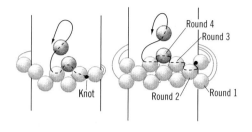

Knot

Round 4
Round 3

Round 2
Round 1

Tubular

Tubular peyote stitch follows the same stitching pattern as flat peyote, but instead of sewing back and forth, you work in rounds.

1 Start with an even number of beads in a ring.

2 Sew through the first bead in the ring. Pick up a bead, skip a bead in the ring, and sew through the next bead. Repeat to complete the round.

3 You need to step up to be in position for the next round. Sew through the first bead added in round 3. Pick up a bead, and sew through the second bead in round 3. Repeat to achieve the desired length.

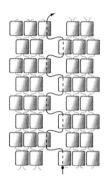

Zipping up or joining

To zip up (join) two sections of a flat peyote piece invisibly, match up the two end rows and zigzag through the up-beads on both ends.

Fig. 1

Fig. 2

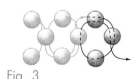

Fig. 3

RIGHT-ANGLE WEAVE

Flat strip

1 To start the first row of right-angle weave, pick up four beads, and tie them into a ring (see "Square knot"). Sew through the first three beads again.

2 Pick up three beads. Sew through the last bead in the previous stitch **(a–b)**, and continue through the first two beads picked up in this stitch **(b–c)**.

3 Continue adding three beads per stitch until the first row is the desired length.

You are stitching in a figure-8 pattern, alternating the direction of the thread path for each stitch.

Forming a strip into a ring

Exit the end bead of the last stitch, pick up a bead, and sew through the end bead of the first stitch. Pick up a bead, and sew through the end bead of the last stitch. Retrace the thread path to reinforce the join.

RIGHT-ANGLE WEAVE (CONTINUED)

Adding rows

1 To add a row, sew through the last stitch of row 1, exiting an edge bead along one side **(fig. 1)**.

2 Pick up three beads, and sew through the edge bead your thread exited in the previous step **(fig. 2, a–b)**. Continue through the first new bead **(b–c)**.

3 Pick up two beads, and sew back through the next edge bead in the previous row and the bead your thread exited at the start of this step **(fig. 3, a–b)**. Continue through the two new beads and the following edge bead in the previous row **(b–c)**.

4 Pick up two beads, and sew through the last two beads your thread exited in the previous stitch and the first new bead. Continue working a figure-8 thread path, picking up two beads per stitch for the rest of the row **(fig. 4)**.

Fig. 1

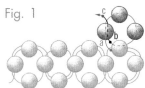

Fig. 2

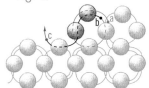

Fig. 3

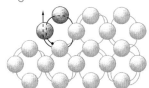

Fig. 4

Tubular

1 Work a flat strip of right-angle weave that is one stitch shorter than needed for the desired circumference of the tube. Form the strip into a ring, exiting an edge bead in the connecting stitch.

2 Add rounds, picking up three beads in the first stitch, two beads in the subsequent stitches, and one bead in the final stitch to join the first and last stitches in the round.

Cubic

In cubic right-angle weave, each cube has six surfaces—four sides, a top, and a bottom. Each surface is made up of four beads, but since the beads are shared, 12 beads are used to make the first cube, and only eight beads are used for each cube thereafter.

To begin the first cube, work three right-angle weave stitches. Join the first and last stitches to form a ring: Pick up a bead, sew through the end bead in the first stitch **(fig. 1, a–b)**, pick up a bead, and sew through the end bead in the last stitch **(b–c)**.

Fig. 2 shows a three-dimensional view of the resulting cube. To make the cube more stable, sew through the four beads on the top of the cube **(fig. 3)**. Sew through the beadwork to the bottom of the cube, and sew through the four remaining beads.

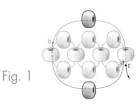

Fig. 1

Fig. 2

Fig. 3

ABOUT**ANNA**

Anna Elizabeth Draeger is a well-known jewelry designer, former associate editor for *Bead&Button* magazine, and the author of *Crystal Brilliance, Creative Designs Using Shaped Beads, More Great Designs for Shaped Beads,* and *Crystal Play*. Anna was an ambassador for the Create Your Style with Swarovski Elements program, a handpicked worldwide network of artists who are known for their design expertise and passion for teaching. Reach Anna at beadbiz@mac.com, or shop for jewelry and kits at: annaelizabethdraeger.etsy.com.

INDEX

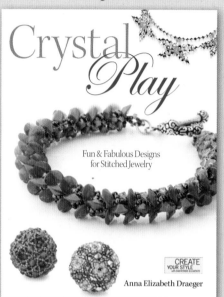
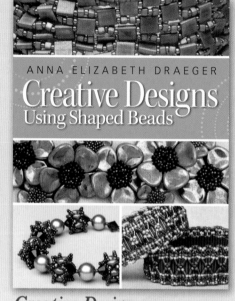
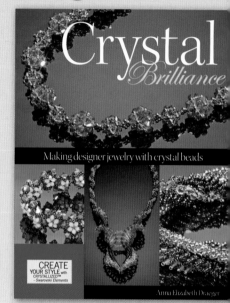